HEGEL ON ART

HEGEL ON ART

AN INTERPRETATION
OF HEGEL'S AESTHETICS

Jack Kaminsky

STATE UNIVERSITY OF NEW YORK PRESS
ALBANY

PUBLISHED BY STATE UNIVERSITY OF NEW YORK PRESS
THURLOW TERRACE, ALBANY, NEW YORK 12201

COPYRIGHT © 1962 BY THE RESEARCH FOUNDATION
OF STATE UNIVERSITY OF NEW YORK, ALBANY, NEW YORK
ALL RIGHTS RESERVED

FIRST PAPERBOUND PRINTING, 1970

STANDARD BOOK NUMBER 87395-065-8
LIBRARY OF CONGRESS CATALOG CARD NUMBER 61-14335
MANUFACTURED IN THE UNITED STATES OF AMERICA

To Alice

Introduction

Modern philosophers have criticized Hegel's philosophy severely. They have generally repudiated his political as well as his metaphysical doctrines. Except for occasional attempts at vindication by Croce, Stace, Mure, and several contemporary European philosophers, thinkers have used Hegel's views to illustrate the hazards of uncontrolled speculation. American and British philosophers especially have deplored not only his linguistic and conceptual obscurity, but also his notorious totalitarian conclusions. Whereas the nineteenth century gloried in the Hegelian teaching, the twentieth century has rejected it.

There are several reasons why the Hegelian philosophy has come perilously close to attaining the status of an interesting but useless historical relic. Because his style is so diffuse, Hegel has been accused of obscurantism. In view of the recent emphasis on the tools of logic and language, contemporary thinkers have made short shrift of the ambiguities inherent in Hegel's exposition of the dialectical process. Philosophers have also reacted strongly to the fascistic implications of his theories. His admiration of the strong state and his idealization of the heroic man have made his philosophy extremely unpopular in an age in which the superman concept has been influential in causing two wars. As a result, little effort has been made to determine whether some portions of the Hegelian philosophy might be salvaged.

In particular, Hegel's aesthetics has been treated most shab-
bily. Unlike other parts of his work, it has not even been
subjected to the kind of strict analysis which should precede
the act of rejection. Usually it has been dismissed as a vain
attempt to stipulate a deterministic evolutionary procedure for
art. The charge of fatalism has inhibited thinkers from undertaking the wearisome task of deciphering Hegel's language.
Hence, there is little real knowledge about his aesthetics beyond the general acquaintance with the notion of the three
stages of art and the Idea that in some nebulous way unravels
in them. There is little familiarity with some of Hegel's dis-
cerning observations and comments about specific works of
art and fundamental aesthetic questions. Yet these detailed
observations are of the sort which would most interest contemporary students of aesthetics. We may no longer be satisfied
with the Hegelian Absolute, or Idea, but this does not detract
from the incisiveness of Hegel's remarks about the nature of
the action in a drama and the organization in a painting.

In this book, therefore, I should like to open inquiry into
Hegel's philosophy of art. I am aware that it is almost impossible to do justice to the richness of his thought in a work as
short as this one. Several objections will be raised by those who
have read his lectures on aesthetics—that various important
insights have been neglected, for instance, or that some profound generalizations have been slighted. But my aim here is
very modest. I am primarily concerned with presenting the
main principles of Hegel's theory of art with the hope of
stimulating an interest in a seminal work on art. If I have
frequently omitted reference to much of the Hegelian metaphysics, it is not because the Hegelian picture of reality is not
worthy of consideration, but because I believe (1) the traditional objections to this picture are valid, and (2) Hegel's
observations about the arts can be appreciated without entail-
ing a commitment to his ontology. Thus, I have written this
book for all who have wondered whether Hegel's views on art
can have any meaning for a highly skeptical and critical

generation. For this reason, much historical material has also been omitted. Sufficient histories of philosophy abound which show Hegel's importance from an historical perspective.

For special help in making this book possible I am indebted to the American Council of Learned Societies for granting me a Fellowship during 1951-1952; to the Research Foundation of the State University of New York for making funds available for publication; to Mrs. Ruth Bellamy, of University Publishers, for her cogent editorial advice; and to Professor Bernard F. Huppé and my wife for their many helpful suggestions.

JACK KAMINSKY

Contents

HEGEL ON ART

I. THE IDEA

BECAUSE Hegel's philosophy of fine art is based not only on his observation of art works and techniques but also on his theory of reality, it is necessary to understand Hegel's metaphysics in order to attain a clear comprehension of his aesthetic theory. A detailed, complete explication of the Hegelian analysis of reality would require a much more ambitious undertaking than this modest volume. However, in this chapter I will outline the Hegelian metaphysics in order to indicate (1) the role that art plays for Hegel in human affairs, and (2) why Hegel's system requires the existence of art.

Perhaps the most important notion to understand in Hegel's theory is the concept which he called the *Idea,* for it is the Idea which gives art its subject matter and its meaningfulness. The *Philosophy of Fine Art* contains several careful explications of the connotation to be attributed to the Idea, but the fuller and more precise attempt at definition is to be found in the two works on logic, the *Science of Logic* and the *Encyclopedical Logic*.[1]

In the works on logic Hegel not only attempts to show how logical forms gradually evolve out of experience, but he also gives us a full account of the problems that gradually forced him to include such a term as Idea in his system. Primarily these problems arise out of some dilemmas and ambiguities that Kant had left as a heritage to his disciples. First of all, one serious puzzle arose because of Kant's espousal of a unique dualism. He had argued for the existence of two sorts of reality. On the one hand, there is that of which we are immediately aware and which Kant called "phenomena" or "experience." This reality is of a very curious sort since its formation is almost completely dependent upon the kind of mind that human beings possess. The world of which we are aware is permeated by space and time, but these formal aspects of our perception are necessarily imposed upon perception by ourselves. We describe the world in terms of objects, properties, and relations, but this description occurs because the cognitive faculties of human beings contain the categories of substance, accident, and causality. In short, we have no right to believe that the world would remain the same if human minds were nonexistent. Another entity with a different type of mind might not perceive things at all in the way we do. But Kant cautions us not to be unduly skeptical about the possibility of obtaining absolutely certain knowledge. Such knowledge can be obtained if we simply recognize our limitations and analyze the experience that is presented to us. We fall into error and skepticism only when we attempt to speak about matters that are inherently nonexperiential.

Kant recognized, however, that if experience were the only reality, then solipsism would be the only philosophy worth believing. If the world man encounters is the kind of world it is because of the mind that he happens to have, then everything to which he ascribes existence exists because of his mind. Destroy his mind and the world is destroyed. This conclusion Kant sought to avoid, and he therefore posited a second reality, the world of "noumena," or things-in-themselves. The noumena for Kant were the realities that were present prior to their conversion by the forms and categories of the human mind. They were what entities would be like if they had not undergone the transformations of space and time and the categories. They were the Lockean substance—unknown but indubitable.

By positing these noumena Kant avoided the pitfalls of

solipsism and subjective idealism. But at the same time he introduced a difficulty that was to plague all the later idealists of the nineteenth century. If knowledge of the world can only be knowledge of the world of phenomena, then how can we be permitted to speak of entities that cannot partake of such a world? In fact, Kant sometimes spoke of these entities as if they were many in number and as if they caused the content of experience to be precisely what it is. But how could these categories, Plurality and Causality—which Kant had specifically claimed could apply only to spatio-temporal phenomena—apply to what was outside the forms of space and time?[2]

A second problem arose in connection with the categories themselves. Kant had described twelve categories which were supposed to form the structure of experience. But Kant's explanation of the principle that governed the deduction of the categories was not satisfactory. Furthermore, Kant had not indicated why twelve and only twelve categories were required. It was not sufficient to argue that these intrinsic structures did in fact permeate the experiences of human beings. This type of psychological argument could not validate Kant's belief that such structures were *necessary* if experience was to occur. Something can be common to experience without being necessary to it. Furthermore, Kant's view that experience is not possible without such structures is also a psychological argument and, therefore, unwarranted. Kant asserted that we cannot *think away* the categories and the forms of space and time. But the fact that we cannot think away a given concept does not make the concept necessary. We may have been trained from childhood to use the concept; it may have certain emotional implications which prohibit our ability to reject it. It may be necessary to us in a psychological but not a logical sense.

Finally, Kant's endeavor to show that the categories were derived from the judgments employed in ordinary formal logic was also unsatisfactory.[3] Kant had, for example, asserted that his category of Unity was a derivation from the purely universal judgment found in logic. Since thinking requires the logical form "all X is Y," the mind must employ concepts of Wholeness and of Unity. Similarly, the presence in our logic of categorical judgments like "X is Y" where X takes proper names as values seemed to Kant to point to the need for the mind to operate in terms of individuals and properties, i.e., the categories of Substance and Accident.[4] All the categories were inferred in this way from the various judgments in the traditional logic.

However, this attempt to show the necessity of admitting specific structures into experience gave rise to two objections. (1) Kant had not adequately analyzed how statements about the categories could be inferred from statements of logic. The statements that denoted the categories were synthetic a priori; the statements of logic were analytic a priori. How could an analytic a priori judgment give rise to a synthetic a priori one? What assertion of formal logic, for example, allows the deduction of "every effect must have a cause"? (2) Even if there were some way of inferring categories from logic, the major aspect of the problem would still not be resolved. Inquiry would have to be directed towards an explanation of the origin and necessity of formal logic itself.[5] Why should the axioms of traditional logic be considered the only ones that can properly be employed in all thinking? "If thought is to be capable of proving anything at all," Hegel declared, "if logic must insist upon the necessity of proofs, and if it proposes to teach the theory of demonstration, its first care should be to give a reason for its own subject-matter, and to see that it is necessary."[6]

The necessary existence of the categories, therefore, had not been proved. And, as a result, two alternatives presented themselves to the followers of Kant. Either Kant's entire transcendental scheme was to be rejected on the grounds that it had not really answered Hume's objections, or else a search was to be made for some yet undiscovered principle whose necessity in experience could not be questioned and from which all the categories could be deduced.[7] Hegel, along with Fichte and

Schelling, accepted the second alternative. As will be seen, the search for this principle led Hegel to the construction of his own philosophy with its concept of the Idea.

Finally, a third major objection was directed against Kant. Kant had maintained that the only knowledge available to us was that derived from the phenomenal, not the noumenal, world. However, our minds do not always function in the most appropriate way. We recognize that there are noumena, but instead of admitting that we can know nothing about this domain of reality, we attempt to ask the same questions of it as we do of the phenomenal world. Since we find general laws in the phenomenal world, we expect to find general laws that will hold for both the noumenal and the phenomenal worlds. As a result, we are gradually led to ask questions concerning the origins of the universe and the nature of the Being that created it. We attempt to apply to noumena the categories that can only be legitimately used with phenomena. When this occurs, Kant explained, we suddenly find ourselves involved in all sorts of curious dilemmas. We find ourselves able to prove that the world was created in time and also that it was not created in time. We can prove that there are indivisible eternal substances and also that there are no indivisible eternal substances. Such contradictions, Kant asserted, can never be resolved because the questions that were originally asked were not really legitimate. We can ask questions about phenomena, but all questions about noumena will lead us to contradictions. Human reason, therefore, oversteps itself as soon as it attempts to formulate positive conclusions about such noumenal matters as the soul, the universe, and God.

However, even Kant had recognized that there were some features of experience that seemed to require the existence of specific noumena. The fact that human beings are involved in moral situations, for example, seemed to imply—even if no proof could be given—that God existed. Thus, although no direct information could be obtained about the noumenal world, some inferences about it seemed to be possible. In short, assuming there is a noumenal world, we could not be so ignorant about it as Kant believed.

In the light of these three general objections Hegel supplied four revisions of the Kantian views:

1. Kant seemed to think that the limitations of human reason were revealed by the seemingly irresolvable contradictions and dilemmas regarding questions about the soul, the universe, and God. But Hegel argued that contradictions were involved in every inquiry that reason conducted.[8] In the most immediate observation there is implicit what is not observable. When we see a table we are also aware that in the same observation there is that which is not a table. But reason is not content with this apparent contradiction. Reason resolves the contradiction by making explicit the law that things cannot be both A and not-A at the same time and in the same respect. Similarly, the fact that questions about the soul, the universe, and God lead to contradictions is not sufficient to make such questions spurious. It might very well be that the philosophic scheme which will resolve such contradictions remains to be found.

2. Kant had limited the powers of reason because he believed that it was invalid to deduce nonempirical conclusions from empirical data. But Hegel reiterated his thesis that the very essence of knowledge is to go from the observable to the non-observable, from the immediate to the mediate, from the explicit to the implicit. We use phenomena in order to gain insight into natural laws which are themselves never observable.

3. Kant may have been right in declaring that without the twelve categories there could be no human experience. But he was wrong in believing that these twelve exhausted all the necessary features that characterized experience. The concept of Becoming, for example, was also required in the description of experience. To distinguish the real from the unreal, the concept of Concrete was also needed. Furthermore, Kant had a mistaken view of the occurrence of structure in experience.

He believed that all the necessary features are given as soon as experience occurs. But just as the essence of the acorn steadily unfolds until the oak is reached, so also the necessary features in experience unfold as experience continues. Not only the body evolves, but experience as well. At any given moment in the evolution of body additional characteristics have still to appear which are part of the essence, or form, of the body. Similarly, at any given moment in the evolution of experience further characteristics (categories) have still to occur which are part of the essence, or form, of experience. For this reason Kant's categories were only a small portion of the truth. They were descriptions of the necessary features that experience possessed at a given moment, not of the features it could possess once it had realized all potentialities. A more inclusive and thorough account of the categories was required.

4. Finally, Hegel who, unlike Kant, had strong ties to the arts believed that Kant's position made the arts cognitively meaningless. For Kant, cognitive judgments referred either to the structure or the content of experience. But what was to be done with judgments such as "X is beautiful"? Kant had argued that the predicate "beautiful" was not to be equated with any scientific predicate. In fact, he explicitly stated that all attempts to turn aesthetic judgments into scientific or empirical ones were doomed to failure. Aesthetic judgments were to be regarded as referring to a very special kind of feeling— the harmony of the cognitive faculties—which occurs when certain specific objects are presented to the senses. In short, Hegel pointed out, Kant was making the aesthetic judgment strictly subjective. Whereas the statements of science refer to phenomena which are at least in some mysterious way attached to noumena, the statements of aesthetics refer strictly to human feelings. The predicate "beautiful" is to be used to indicate the emotion that is aroused when a given object appears; it is not a description of a property of the object.

Hegel, however, was convinced that a more thorough examination of the categories would show that the predicate "beautiful" had as much application as has any other predicate. As experience evolves, religious as well as aesthetic concepts become necessary means by which experience is made intelligible.

Hegel, therefore, had some very serious reservations about the Kantian philosophy. He agreed that Kant was the first philosopher to deal with the ways in which the human mind creates its own reality, but felt that he had left too much unexplained. He had not dealt adequately with the categories and, because of the resultant restrictions on knowledge, had been forced to eliminate aesthetics as a genuine area of knowledge. What was demanded, therefore, was a full-scale revision of the Kantian analysis which would show (1) that Kant's restrictions on knowledge were too severe, and (2) that a more liberal definition of knowledge could include the aesthetic judgment.

The problem of the categories, consequently, became the starting point for Hegel's own philosophy. Was there some method—some logical tool—by which the necessity of the categories could be demonstrated and the complete list of the categories discovered? Kant had simply listed the categories, but this procedure was as objectionable as the mere listing of the theorems of geometry without showing their derivation from the axioms. Where was a principle (or a set of principles) and a warranted rule of inference to be found by means of which the appropriate deductions could be made?

Fichte had supplied a clue to the answer. He had argued that two self-evident propositions can be posited: "there is an I" and "there is a non-I." The I can be regarded as simple awareness of unity among all diversity or as an internal principle of organization. The non-I can be defined as awareness of an external element or of an element which is distinct from any internal principle of organization. The non-I acts as a "resistance stimulus" (*Anstöss*) which causes the I to respond.[9] The response consists of an endeavor to mold what is external into a form to which the internal principle of organization is applicable. In simple terms, Fichte believed that experience, with all its required categories, evolved as mind and environment reacted to one another. Thus, by analyzing what mind does in giving rational form to external data, we should begin to see how the categories develop in experience. Like an art work that gradually attains form as the artist molds and remolds his clay, experience attains form as man reacts to a constantly changing environment. The necessary features of experience can be deduced, Fichte believed, if we simply analyze how mind tries to overcome an unfriendly and alien environment. Each feature serves to make the environment less alien and more adaptable to human control.

Hegel sympathized with Fichte's views. But he believed that Fichte's resistance-stimulus appeared to be no more than Kant's noumena in disguise. It was true that Fichte's philosophy presented a possible way of accounting for the existence of the particular categories that were to be found in experience. But the solution was based on a dichotomy that had already been deemed untenable. Furthermore, Fichte had not presented a principle of inference by which one could show how categories logically followed from one another. The conflict between mind and environment might initiate the categories, but it did not tell us what mind did in producing them and relating them to prior ones.

What, then, is to be done? First of all, Hegel declares, Fichte was wrong in believing that "there is an I" is grasped as an immediate truth by any mind. The conception of an I is by no means the first conception that the mind entertains. Fichte, like Descartes, had used the wrong starting point in his philosophy. The conception of an Ego is really a sophisticated conception that is derivable from more basic grounds. Only gradually do we recognize ourselves as distinct entities divorced from all other entities.

Where, then, is the legitimate beginning? Hegel maintained that there is one notion which is primary to all others and appears at the very first presentation of conscious thought:

the conception of Being. The very least that we can say about anything that appears is that it has being. Such a category is implicit in every inquiry into experience. We must at least say that experience *is*. This does not mean that we are identifying what Being is. To assert that there is something does not commit us to asserting what that something is. The concept of Being simply indicates the earliest recognition that we are undergoing experience. Hegel was aware that temporally the category of Being may be recognized much later than other categories, such as Causation. But logically Being is prior, since the positing of any other category, according to Hegel, presupposes the category of Being. That phenomena are present, therefore, is the primary self-evident fact. According to Hegel, it satisfies that condition which any axiom must satisfy if it is to be the foundation of a deductive system. The foundation "must be an absolute, or, what here is equivalent, an abstract beginning; it must presuppose nothing, must be mediated by nothing, must have no foundations: itself is to be the foundation of the whole science."[10]

It should be noted that Hegel, at this stage of his presentation, did not say that anything exists; in fact, he was not yet even saying that there are any determinate things. McTaggart is quite misleading when he states that "the only logical postulate which the dialectic requires is the admission that experience really exists."[11] Existence is a category which Hegel sharply distinguished from the primary category of Being.[12] We can, according to Hegel, logically conceive of the very first presentation of experience in which it would only be permissible to say that experience is. Only later do we differentiate between the class whose members exist and the class whose members do not exist. At this point Hegel was simply selecting what he believed would admittedly be the very least that could be said about any experience.

Hegel was aware that the mere assertion that Being is the first concept that can define experience was not a novel statement in philosophy. Parmenides had also maintained that the concept of Being is logically first in any attempt to define what is given. The crucial problem was, what more could be said besides the mere fact that Being is applicable to experience? Parmenides had been unable to prove anything further. He began with Being and remained with Being. He did not present any method by which further concepts could be derived. In Hegelian terms, Parmenides' universal was abstract and not concrete. For this reason his philosophy seemed to Hegel to be negativistic and sterile. To Hegel the category of Being was dynamic.[13] It entailed other concepts. To prove this belief became his major philosophic task.

When we speak of a state of affairs that has being only, we mean a state which is simply indeterminate and without any specifiable characteristics. The admission of determinate entities and characteristics could only come later, when mind begins to make distinctions in the mere givenness of experience. At this stage that we are now considering, however, there is nothing to identify in experience. It is "the original featurelessness which precedes all definite character and is the very first of all."[14] Hegel was aware that experience as we perceive it is not a blank at all and that we perceive things, colors, and so forth. We can, however, logically conceive of a state in which we do not perceive things as things, or colors as colors. In such a case only a blank indeterminateness would prevail in our consciousness. If it were possible to define this very first category, we would describe it as pure vacuity. In fact, our definition would be identical with the kind of definition we would give if we were called upon to define such an abstract term as "Nothing." Being, Hegel declared, "is pure indeterminateness and vacuity. Nothing can be intuited in it, if there is any question here of intuition, or again it is merely this pure and empty intuition itself; equally there is in it no object for thought, or again it is just this empty thought. In fact, Being, indeterminate immediacy, is Nothing, neither more nor less."[15]

It is important to recognize the full import of Hegel's conclusions. He was not only stating that both X and non-X refer to the same state of affairs, Y.[16] He was also claiming that thought is such at this stage of cognition that the use of one term to describe experience immediately produces the opposite of that term. One concept has entailed another concept. Hegel recognized that this simple entailment of Nothing by Being is not particularly pertinent to the problem of making experience intelligible. Both categories are much too abstract. But he believed it proved something very important about the nature of the human mind. The human mind has the unusual power of analyzing in terms of opposites. As soon as it entertains one concept it immediately must deal with the exact opposite of that concept. We cannot just think of Being; we must also think of Nothing.

To say "there is an X" and X has some meaning commits us to a belief in the statement "there is a Y" such that Y is identical to *non-X*. Hegel, we shall see, often confused contraries with contradictories. He sometimes identified *non-X* with a term that really had a contrary relation to X. For this reason many of his deductions turned out to be invalid. To say "Y is non-red," for example, is not equivalent to asserting "Y is blue." But at least at this early point in his argument Hegel is maintaining simply that there is an inherent disposition in the mind, namely, its disposition to negate any proposition it formulates.

Some very obvious objections can be raised against Hegel's deduction. But it is to his credit that he sought to answer most of them. Thus he realized that this identification of Being and Nothing can be interpreted crudely, and he presented a number of arguments to absolve himself of the charge that he was violating the law of contradiction.[17] It is important to remember, Hegel stated, that in its early stages consciousness has not yet been presented with a characteristic by means of which a distinction between Nothing and Being can be made. The presentation of such a characteristic has still to be achieved.

At this stage only the bare abstract concepts are involved. It would be as if we became aware that the propositional form "all X is Y" can be changed into the obverted negative form "no X is *non-Y*." The law of contradiction begins to apply only when the category of Entity becomes a necessary structure of experience. Only when we speak of things can we say that two contradictory properties cannot apply to the same thing at the same time and in the same respect. In typical Aristotelian fashion Hegel argues that properties have meaning only insofar as they attach to things. But if we talk about an experience in which the category of things has not yet been employed, then the law of contradiction is not yet applicable. There are no things to which the law can apply. Therefore, no contradiction is involved in the contention that experience in its initial stage is characterized by both Being and Nothing.

With this explication Hegel defends his belief that mind is a basically dynamic substance which posits Being and then immediately introduces the denial of Being, Nothing. This is the first step of what has been called the dialectical process of reasoning. But the dialectical process is not completed. Mind does more than bring negation into judgments. It also demands that some further concept be produced to unify, or mediate, the dichotomy of affirmation and negation. Mind stimulates the search for concepts which will resolve any apparent contradictions in experience.

Thus there arises a new concept—one which shows that Being and Nothing are actually compatible. In this case the new concept is Becoming. Becoming signifies an experience that is and yet is not. For example, when something is in the process of becoming, it is at once precisely what it is but at the same time it is not what it has still to become. Becoming, in the language of the Hegelian dialectician, produces a synthesis out of the thesis, Being, and the antithesis, Nothing.

Thus, for Hegel, the term "dialectic" indicates an inherent power that the human mind brings to every subject matter. Every affirmative proposition implies its own denial and the resultant contradiction implies some further proposition which will eliminate the contradiction. But the elimination of a contradiction means that a new proposition has been posited and this in turn becomes negated. Thus, for example, the concept of Becoming eliminates the apparent contradiction between Being and Nothing.

The first dialectic triad is Being, Nothing, and Becoming. But the negating characteristic of the human mind does not cease to function once Becoming has been reached. The dialectic process now begins anew. A negation to Becoming now appears. This negation turns out to be Determinate Being. Something which is determinate is not becoming. But this first step of the dialectic process is always followed by the second step. Mind is now once again in the process of entertaining a thesis, Becoming, and an antithesis, Determinate Being, and as a result a new synthesis is required. What concept can account for the contradiction between Becoming and Determinate Being, or, in other words, between change and permanence? Hegel answers that the contradiction between Becoming and Determinate Being is overcome when we posit the category of Quality. Something is what it is—i.e., it is determinate—when it can be defined by a particular quality or set of qualities. When the entity changes or becomes different, we mean that these qualities have been replaced by others. Thus, to say that a determinate being is becoming is to say, in Aristotelian fashion, that a new quality has appeared in a permanent substance. The contradiction between permanence (Determinate Being) and change (Becoming) is no longer present. Another dialectic triad is completed.

It is not necessary to give in detail the entire Hegelian logic as it develops from the category of Being. Each completed triad produces a new negation and each new negation results in a new synthesis. Gradually all the necessary features of experience are exhibited, including those listed by Kant. And finally the most inclusive category of all is deduced, viz., the Absolute Idea.

Before we begin our analysis of the Absolute Idea several remarks ought to be made concerning the dialectic process that Hegel has made so critical a part of his philosophy. First of all, in spite of Hegel's insistence that the dialectical method does not violate the law of contradiction, there is an important sense in which it does. Hegel argues that given the concept Being, the concept Nothing is automatically deduced. He insists that he has deduced no more than a synonym for Being. We define Being and Nothing in the same way, according to Hegel. But if this is the case, then Being and Nothing *are* identical. The term Nothing is, therefore, not functioning in the way that it normally does, namely, as part of a denial of some statement. Hegel is simply positing another term, Nothing, as a synonym for the term Being.

Why, then, does Hegel believe that he has deduced the contradictory of Being? Largely because he has confused two meanings of the word Nothing. He begins by giving the same definition to Being and Nothing. As we have seen, they both refer to the same indeterminateness and vacuity. By stipulation the term Nothing is thus to be taken as a synonym for the term Being, with no contradiction present. Hegel simply permits a new term to be an allowable substitute for another term. However, in normal usage Nothing is taken to mean the contradictory of Being, in which case there is a contradiction, not an identity. Nothing and Being do *not* describe the same phenomena. What Hegel has done is to confuse a stipulated with a conventional meaning of a word. He stipulates that the word "Nothing" is to mean the same as "Being" and then surreptitiously or unwittingly inserts the meaning of "Nothing" which is used in everyday language. By fiat he introduces a new word, but this does not mean he has also changed the meaning that word is normally taken to have.

Secondly, Hegel claims that his deductions refer to necessary characteristics in experience. The categories refer to specific positive features in experience. Thus the contradictories that Hegel must deduce must be describable in an affirmative, not a negative, statement. For example, to say that X is not green does not tell us what color X actually is. For this reason Hegel's contradictories frequently turn out to be contraries. The contradiction of Becoming is Non-Becoming but Hegel, in order to make the category positive, substitutes Determinate Being for Non-Becoming. He deduces what is actually a contrary even though he is only justified in deducing a contradictory.

Thus, even though Hegel may be right in arguing that there are some terms whose meaning entails the addition of further predicates, his dialectic method is not sufficient to uphold this view. He might be able to give a psychological reason for arguing that X involves its contradictory, non-X. But only if non-X could be shown to be equivalent to some contrary Y would it be possible to argue that there is some third concept Z from which X and Y are deducible. Unfortunately, Hegel does not show how contradictories lead to the assertion of contraries.

There are weaknesses, therefore, in the Hegelian scheme.[18] But if Hegel had been able to argue for the deduction of contraries, then it is not too difficult to understand how he might finally have derived his last and, at least for him, most significant category, the Absolute Idea.

Perhaps the best way to understand the Absolute Idea is to think of it as being analogous to the Aristotelian final end.[19] Aristotle had maintained that change can be explained only in terms of a final *telos*. For example, to explain the change in an acorn one must consider the oak which the acorn is to become. All natural objects aim at the realization of some end. And that there are such ends is due to the fact that there is one Final End called the Unmoved Mover.

Aristotle's teleology is derived primarily from his observation of nature. For him teleology is an objective fact in the natural world. But when we turn to Hegel we find an entirely new philosophic orientation. Hegel, like most of the idealist philosophers of the nineteenth century, rejects the dichotomy between nature and experience. For him experience is as totally teleological as Aristotle's nature.

For this reason the Absolute Idea can be equated with the Unmoved Mover. But whereas the Unmoved Mover is the source of motion for natural objects, the Absolute Idea is the source of motion in experience. If we employ Aristotelian terminology, we can say that the Absolute Idea is to be equated with the efficient and final causes of all the changes in experience from infancy to maturity. The acorn grows into an oak; the experience of infancy develops into maturity. The very fact that such development occurs is evidence of the Absolute Idea. If there were no underlying force of this kind, there would be no way of accounting for the fact that we actively try to overcome contradictions and develop potentialities we believe we have. Hegel repeatedly insists that the Absolute Idea functions as a telic agent in all human endeavor. It causes us to search continually for more embracing ways of explaining sense observations. It makes us assume that every phenomenon can finally be described in some all-inclusive system. Just as the exclusion of the essence in the instance of the acorn would make it impossible for us to explain why the acorn evolves precisely the way that it does, so also without the Absolute Idea there would be no way of accounting for the fact that all of us are actively engaged in resolving problems and inquiries. The Absolute Idea is the hidden form that seeks to obtain full realization in the matter of experience. It is the hidden standard which causes us to ask whether a given explanation is *really* satisfactory, or whether a proposed hypothesis will *really* work. The Absolute Idea is the motivating principle which makes us accept logic as an instrument of knowledge and which makes the construction of calculi and the deduction of theorems seem to be meaningful activities. If a man were born without this motivating principle, his experience would be no more than a wild chaotic flash of light and sound. There would be no right or wrong, good or bad, correct or incorrect. There could be no expectations or anticipations because only a mind which has a conception of fulfillment could undergo an expectation or an anticipation. In short, it is because human experience does contain these implicit dispositions that it *is* what we know as human experience.

The dialectic pattern that thinking follows is a manifestation of the Absolute Idea. The dialectic is the logic by which the Absolute Idea finally expresses itself. The very fact that mind does not stop simply with Being is because of the inherent need of mind to make explicit what is only implicit in it. The category of Nothing must be posited because (1) the implicit Absolute Idea forces mind to posit other categories, and (2) the logic of negation, the dialectic, requires that the next category be the contradiction of Being.

With this understanding of the Absolute Idea we can better understand the rationale for the development of Hegel's categories from Being to the Absolute Idea. Again, using the Aristotelian analogy, the Absolute Idea can be compared to the full development of the acorn. It can be equated with the full appearance of the oak. The difference consists in the fact that for Hegel the interval between Being and the Absolute Idea takes in every type of knowledge with which men have ever dealt. We do not accidentally become involved in scientific inquiry; each step of the dialectic serves to initiate further activity on the part of man. The hidden laws of the part of experience called Nature are gradually revealed to us as the Absolute Idea unravels itself in human consciousness. Similarly, it is no mere accident that religion and art are elements of experience. These also play their particular roles in bringing the Absolute Idea to explicit realization.

If art and religion are subjective then so also, according to Hegel, are physics and the other sciences. Each area of knowledge is an aspect of the Absolute Idea in the same way that each stage in the development of the acorn is a manifestation of the oak. Some parts of knowledge may show more of the Absolute —in the same way we can tell more about the oak when it is near its final stages of development—but this does not mean that in some way one kind of knowledge is less objective than another kind. Art may not have the precision of physics but, according to Hegel, it has as crucial a role in revealing to us an aspect of the Idea.

As the dialectic process continues, two important concepts appear in experience, namely, self-consciousness and nature. With the advent of this dichotomy a new phase begins for human inquiry. Introspection as well as the study of nature become highly significant investigations. But the investigations do not consist in the mere listing of data. On the contrary, there is now a general awareness that a rational pattern is present in experience and that a full explication of this pattern is required. This explication proceeds in two steps.

First of all, inquiry is directed towards the external world. The examination of nature becomes the first important step for giving an adequate linguistic and mathematical expression of the rational pattern that permeates experience. Thus Hegel points out the curious hierarchy to be found in nature. When we compare inanimate to animate things and when, furthermore, we investigate animate things themselves, we find, according to Hegel, ample evidence for believing that some inherent force gradually evolves from the simplest state of being to the most complex. Some inanimate things, for example, can be described as primarily aggregates. They are no more than a cluster of material particles without any unifying relationship. Such clusters occur by accident and disappear by accident. But if inquiry continues long enough, it encounters some inanimate entities whose parts are not mere clusters. The parts are not indifferent to one another, but, on the contrary, are affected by one another. To account for this new phenomenon, mind employs a new concept designated by the term "affinity." This concept attempts to explain the various chemical occurrences which are so sharply differentiated from mere aggregate substances.[20] With the recognition of affinity comes the first recognition of a unique unifying power. Particular independent entities, revealing a peculiar mutual preference, are seen to be fused into a whole in which the

characteristics of the parts are obliterated by the characteristics of the whole. The bringing together of certain kinds
of elements produces a transformation which cannot be
accounted for by the mechanical laws that govern the simplest
inanimate objects.

However, the unity studied in chemistry is only a small and
partial manifestation of the underlying Idea. There are more
revealing exhibitions. The chemism of atomic structure is not
comparable to the vitalistic component that is found in other
structures. It is, therefore, in that phenomenon which we
designate by the term "life" that the unique principle which
only suggested itself in the chemical process begins to freely
exhibit itself. Not only is there a more intimate unity of the
parts,[21] but the whole is also now qualified by activities designed to keep the unity intact. The chemical process may have
signified the fusion of parts, but it is not the explicit activity
concerned with maintaining unity against possible external
disunifying forces.

However, life in its earliest form realizes only few of the
potentialities that are implicit in living matter. The characteristics of life in the single cell are to be sharply distinguished
from the characteristics of life in the complex animal. In the
animal the integrative principle has served to give better protection to the vital organs. With the advent of sensation and
perception the reaction to possible disintegration has become
more acute and discriminating. But even in the animal the
potentialities of the life-giving force, of the Absolute Idea,
have not been fully actualized. The animal is still incapable of
anticipating challenges to its equilibrium. Even in those cases
where such anticipation does seem to occur, there is no capacity
for correct evaluation of what would most adequately restore
equilibrium or prevent its destruction.

Only one animal comes close to realizing the potentialities
that are implicit in life—namely, man. He alone exemplifies
the kind of potentiality that the Idea strives to realize in

matter. For Hegel, then, as for Aristotle, man is at the apex of the hierarchy.

When we attempt to define what man is, however, we find the task is not a simple one. Whereas the ordinary animal can be explained in behavioral and mechanistic terms, analysis of man requires inquiry into an entirely new dimension of phenomena. An explication of man's potentialities demands that we fully investigate his psychological as well as his physical characteristics. According to Hegel, man's *spirit* —his unique way of thinking—is what distinguishes him from all other animals. The potentialities that he can realize are not the simple physical ones. His powers are of a different order. He has an entirely new capacity to exercise and perfect. This is the capacity of thought.

The question therefore arises: What is the function of thought? What is the *telos,* the end, that thought is seeking to make explicit? For Hegel the answer is obvious. The function of thought is to attain a knowledge of the rational structure that permeates all of being. Thought strives to produce self-consciousness and, finally, a full awareness of the place and role of man in the world. When thought reaches this stage it has made explicit everything implicit in the very first appearance of living substance. The acorn has become an oak. Similarly, the rudiments of sense and intelligence in the one-celled animal have evolved into the fully matured sensory and intellectual characteristics of man.

Now we are in a position to determine the role of art in the Hegelian philosophy. In his endeavor to gain a rational knowledge of the world man uses three approaches. First of all, he tries to *image* the rational structure of the world; that is, he tries to organize sensuous data in such a way that the presence of the Idea is recognizable. Out of this endeavor arises Art. The second approach comes from the attempt to display the Idea by means of imagery, symbolism, and allegory. Out of this effort arises Religion. Finally, men begin to construct all-encompassing logical systems which avoid commitments to imagery and allegorical devices. This new inquiry leads to the highest kind of discipline, namely, Philosophy. Only Philosophy is able to demonstrate the rational order which permeates all of being.[22] Thus, for Hegel, art is a necessity in human experience. It is not as complete a manifestation of the Idea as Religion or Philosophy. But it still plays a crucial role in giving man insight into the function of thought and into the *telos* that pervades both mind and matter.

By means of this dialectical view of reality Hegel firmly believed that he had provided the solution for the necessity of the categories and that he had also demonstrated the rationale for art. He was now ready to begin a detailed analysis of art. However, before we examine Hegel's views on art and aesthetic experience, some further comments ought to be made about the Hegelian metaphysics.

Some serious objections can be raised against the Hegelian philosophy. First of all, Hegel's teleological scheme is involved in difficulties that often beset teleological interpretations of nature. The notion of purpose can frequently be used as a two-edged sword. What is a final end to one man can be a beginning to another. In accordance with tradition, Hegel accepts the view that man is the apex of the hierarchy of being. But he is not at the apex by chance or by some process of natural selection. For Hegel, man—or at least beings with rational powers—is the end which nature has been seeking to realize. But this form of teleology is open to the serious charge that a subtle identification has been made between what *is* and what *necessarily is*. Even if it were admitted that the hierarchy described by Hegel (and by Aristotle) did exist, the mere fact of existence would be no guarantee that such an existence was necessary. The fact that there is order is no guarantee that the order could not have been different. Of course, Hegel believed that his dialectic logic guaranteed his teleology. But we have already seen, first, that the logic is applicable only if Hegel can show us how he can obtain contraries from his negations. (He has not done this.) Second, there is a serious question as to whether Hegel's logic is able to demonstrate that *anything at all* exists. The Hegelian categories are such that no deduction of a specific entity is ever made. When Hegel deduces the concept "existent thing" he has not deduced the existence of a specific entity such as "this dog." In fact, we should not think that he has even deduced the existence of a specific class, such as the class of dogs. Hegel's categories, like those of Kant, have the curious characteristic of being able to accommodate themselves to anything in experience. It makes no real difference to the positing of the categories whether there are or are not dogs. Even if all phenomena ceased to be what they are—if, for example, objects began to fall at a slower rate than 32 feet per second per second—the categories would still be valid. In short, the categories require that something must exist, but not that any specific thing must exist. For this reason Hegel cannot really claim that his categories entail the existence of a specific kind of teleology. No matter what kind of world prevailed in the future the categories would still be applicable. But if no experience can ever falsify them, then no specific state of affairs is ever assured by them. Hegel was undoubtedly right when he sought to change abstract universals into concrete ones. But his changes were never so concrete that the existence of specific things was entailed. Yet precisely such an entailment was needed if his teleology was to be justified.[23]

Another serious objection to the Hegelian philosophy deals with an ambiguity in the definition of the Idea. We have been equating the Absolute Idea with the Unmoved Mover. But actually this is not an altogether legitimate comparison. The Unmoved Mover is a real entity that is over and above the substances which it causes to evolve. But the Absolute Idea does not have this separate status. For Aristotle, being in motion implies the existence of being not in motion, the Unmoved Mover. One may disagree with the Aristotelian analysis, but at least his position is clear. There are at least two separate beings in the world—the being we observe and the unobservable Being. A belief in one commits us to a belief in the other. But for Hegel the fact that there is being in motion does not merely imply the existence of the Idea; both the being in motion and the being of the Idea are identical. Hegel very specifically declares that the complete knowledge one finally attains through philosophy is not a knowledge of two things—the world and the Absolute. The relationship between the world and the Idea is not one of created to the creator. Knowledge of the world and of the Idea are one and the same. But if this is the case, then the Idea suddenly becomes a trivial notion in the Hegelian scheme. We can assume Hegel to be arguing that one ought to gain as complete a knowledge as possible of the various relations among and within all subject matters. But by equating this knowledge with the Idea, Hegel has not added any more information than he has already given us. Since "Idea" and "complete knowledge" are identical, the word "Idea" is not very significant. It surely ought not to have been hypostatized by Hegel in all his works.

Perhaps the criticism made above may be presented from a different viewpoint. For Hegel the Idea reaches a stage when its contents have been made explicit; that is to say, when a full and conscious awareness is present of the unity that ties entities together. This state of unity we shall call "X." To explain this explicit presentation of "X" we need some cause. Let us call the cause "Y." Now in other metaphysical schemes "Y" is usually a force of some kind, or an external God, or even a special set of atoms. In most cases "Y" is different from "X." For Hegel, however, 'Y" is the very unity that presents itself. In short, "Y" is identical to "X." The circularity should be apparent. The cause of "X" is "Y" and "Y" is identical to "X."

The metaphysics of Hegel, therefore, is by no means exempt from criticism. But I do not think that these criticisms invalidate Hegel's aesthetic theory. Fortunately, when Hegel descends to particulars the dialectic process is ignored. As we shall see, we can appreciate Hegel's analysis of dramatic action without committing ourselves to the ontology he propounds.

For Hegel, art is a highly important instrument for giving us insight into the nature of the Idea. Art objects are distinguished from ordinary sense objects in that the former are sense objects organized in a specific way. They are deliberately combined in such a way that an observer will become aware that sense phenomena are signs of a more fundamental kind of knowledge. Art, however, is not given to us in a completed fashion. Every area of inquiry, Hegel insists, has a beginning, a middle, and an end. Philosophy begins with the provocative but not fully formed beliefs of the pre-Socratics and Plato, and evolves to the more complete and more thoroughly finished views of Kant and the idealists. Similarly, theology begins with the primitivism found in the early Egyptian culture and matures into the scrupulously wrought symbolism of Christianity. Every field has the same logic by which it develops. Thus for Hegel art also matures out of origins that are primitive and irrational. It begins with Egyptian amateurism and develops into the professional and highly sophisticated work of a Da Vinci and a Tintoretto.

Art, therefore, is a necessity for men because only a few rare individuals are able to overcome their complete reliance on sense imagery. Nor does art arise merely out of practical necessity. There is a logic in the development of human self-consciousness which requires the advent of art. Just as Plato had pointed out in the *Republic* that the attainment of genuine knowledge must be preceded by reliance on sense observation, so also Hegel declares that the gradual development of human consciousness from primitivism to understanding requires art as a necessary step. Only philosophy produces real knowledge. But without art philosophy could not have arisen.

The role of the artist is now quite clear. What makes him an artist is his ability to organize sense objects in such a way that they will serve to call attention to the indicative nature of sense perceptions. If the artist succeeds, then the observer of his work will suddenly see more than the mere imagery; he will also see in an intellectual sense the underlying concept of which the imagery is supposed to be a manifestation. If the artist fails, then no underlying concept has appeared.

II. THE IDEA IN ART

BECAUSE Hegel's theory of art is an essential part of his metaphysics, he rejects the Kantian theory of aesthetics which reduces the appreciation of art to an interesting but not especially necessary adventure for human beings. For Hegel, experience without art is barbaric.

The artistic experience, Hegel will argue, however, is not divorced from its temporal and environmental setting. The Idea—like the Schopenhauerian will—is the force that permeates all living things and makes them evolve spiritually as well as physically. Each successive age produces a little more consciousness of how the Idea manifests itself in spirit and in nature. For this reason the concept of God found in primitive societies is far less comprehensible than the Christian concept of God. Only after centuries of human speculation did the nature of the Idea become revealed to man. The philosophers and scientists of each age brought a little more clarity into the difficult process of making the Idea intelligible to the human mind. The earliest thinkers merely represented the Idea in its most abstract form. They posited a vague, unknown, and undefined Being. For this reason early art is unformed and naïve. It was just as difficult for the artist as for the philosopher to represent some phase of experience which was not yet fully understood. Art evolved as the artist gradually became aware of what it was in experience that he sought to reveal in art. It is to an investigation of this ideal artistic subject matter that we must now turn.

For Hegel, the aesthetic experience is not simply an emotional state without objective counterpart. He would undoubtedly have been shocked by the view of some contemporary philosophers that the term "beautiful" is essentially an emotive one. Hegel would agree that part of the definition of "beautiful" must take cognizance of the fact that a particular kind of elation is occurring.[1] But more is needed in the definition. The causes of such elation must also be included. For Hegel, an aesthetic experience is in many respects analogous to a sensory experience. The sensation of red is not defined simply by referring to the sensation itself but also by referring to the external conditions that produce this sensation. In the same way the definition of "beautiful" ought to contain words indicating both subjective and objective factors. But what are the objective factors? Some objective characteristics which have been listed in the definition of the aesthetic experience Hegel rejects. In Hegel's view, to speak of a great work of art simply in terms of technical flawlessness would only serve to trivialize the importance of art in human culture and would not adequately explain the distinction between the admiration for technique and the genuine aesthetic experience. Nor can the art work be defined in terms of the presence of a given pattern of colors, sounds, or words, which would be to confuse appreciation of technique with aesthetic appreciation. What, then, does "beautiful" mean? Hegel's answer is that "beautiful" designates the presence of a certain kind of relationship which the artist has caused to appear in his work. He is able to bring sounds, words, or colors together in such a unique fashion that a certain highly organized and original relationship makes its appearance to the artist and the observer.

This does not mean that the artist is concerned with communicating scientific knowledge.[2] The relationship he seeks to produce is not reducible to scientific terms. Science describes what nature is; the artist seeks to present what nature is a sign of. The scientist describes mankind; the artist depicts what mankind is trying to become. For this reason the aim of the artist is never one of imitation of existential entities. Art, according to Hegel, is superior to nature. It tries to indicate the goals at which nature is aiming. In art man tries to succeed where nature often fails. In the natural realm man is far from perfect. His potentialities, for the most part, go unrealized and even unnoticed. Art is the instrument by which insight is attained into what it means to be a man. The artist can shape for us the kind of human being we ought to become. In short, the artist tries to show men what kind of man would be the fullest expression of the Idea.

Thus, artists may look to nature for inspiration. But their task is to reconstruct nature so that the richness of the Idea becomes evident. Science is concerned with facts; the artist is concerned with facts and ideals.

The best subject matter for art is, of course, mankind, since man is at the pinnacle of the hierarchy of being. But now Hegel must develop his theory more concretely. Even if man is regarded as the highest development of the Idea, a decided ambiguity remains as to what phase of man is to be artistically represented. Not man per se is the artistic model, for there is much in man that is ugly and brutish. The artist, therefore, must be a keen observer and thinker. He must have the critical ability to distinguish the ideal from the non-ideal, the animalistic from the spiritualistic. He must seek for those moments when man is as he should be, when man becomes what potentially he can become.

However, the crucial question now arises: How are we to distinguish between ideal and non-ideal moments?[3] What characteristics must an action or event or personality have before they can be deemed the highest realization of the Idea?

Hegel points out that human activity attains the status of "ideal" or "noble" on certain special occasions. For example, when a man risks his life in order to assert what he believes is true, then such behavior is often labelled "ideal." In this connection we introduce the word "ought" and say, "That is what a man ought to do." For Hegel, such events are rare but all of them are characterized by conflict involving freedom of thought and the determination to do what is right. But such events—which Hegel has still to examine in greater detail—can occur only under very special conditions. If a society is very rigid, if every activity is carefully controlled by the state or by written law, then the possibility of such events occurring is very slim.[4] In the past, Hegel maintains, when a society was loosely organized, when its laws and conventions were still not codified, then there existed much more of that activity deemed "ideal." The Greek and the early Christian societies realized enormous artistic and intellectual production because in those societies legal and moral systems were not so fully developed and so unpliant that free spiritual and intellectual activity were difficult to maintain. Therefore, to assure a genuine possibility for truly moral action, the social context must be such that it permits change and revision of existent laws and conventions.

This is the first condition—the *General World-Condition,* in Hegel's terminology[5]—which must be present if we are to discover the kind of activity which exhibits man at his best. The importance of this point is twofold. First of all, it indicates that the display of ideal activity is not easy to detect. The artist's endeavor to uncover instances of such behavior is frequently inhibited by the very social context in which he finds himself. For this reason some ages are more productive than others. Secondly, it serves at least to lessen the charge often made against Hegel, that he believed very strongly in authoritarian governments. Hegel recognized that a completely closed type of society would not permit the individualistic kind of activity in which ideal human behavior is possible. The Idea is a process which unravels itself in human personality, and only a society which encourages freedom and contains groups that can act creatively without strict obedience to social conventions is able to make ideal action possible.

The General World-Condition, however, is a necessary but not a sufficient condition for the occurrence of ideal actions. A society might allow individual freedom and still not produce the kind of activity that becomes an exemplar, an ideal, for all future human behavior. It might lack the type of individual who can or who wishes to produce such ideal action. Therefore, the society in which ideal action can take place must contain individuals who recognize and assert their own freedom, who conceive of themselves as being capable of independent and fearless action. Such people, Hegel believes, are usually to be discovered in the upper classes of a society, specifically in the nobility. This class alone has the means and the initiative to undertake tasks demanding the highest ethical conduct. Hegel warned, however, that the selection of the aristocracy of a society as the best representatives of possible ideal action is made not because there is an inherent value in the upper classes but "simply on account of the perfection in which free will and its products may be exemplified . . . through the highly placed class."[6] Thus, ideal action may come from the very lowest classes, but the possibility is remote since these classes are much too burdened by the problems of survival and by an infinite number of ignorant prejudices. Only where individuals act without the fears and prejudices that beset the ordinary man can events attain an ideal status.

However, the sufficient condition for ideal action has not yet been presented. Although ideal actions belong to the class of actions undertaken by the nobility, the mark for distinguishing ideal from non-ideal actions has still not been discovered. It is with the introduction of the *Situation* that the kind of action Hegel wishes to define becomes more specifically circumscribed.[7]

The Situation is an important concept for Hegel, and its clarification is "necessary to any inquiry into the true constituents of *action*."[8] Although Hegel's analysis of the Situation is extremely arduous, if we understand Hegel's procedure to be one of constantly narrowing the class to which ideal actions can belong, the meaning of this new concept will become easier to discern. Ideal actions and events can take place only in a certain kind of social context and only by means of specific types of individuals. But even individuals belonging to the nobility perform inconsequential and meaningless actions. Thus a new criterion must be sought which will separate the ideal from the non-ideal actions of the nobility.

Hegel found this criterion by making a very penetrating analysis of human activity. He began by recalling how erratic and directionless some of the actions of human beings are. But other actions can be described in terms of purposes and means undertaken to accomplish these purposes. In these latter activities a plan appears which is absent in directionless behavior. Mere random motion becomes converted into a series of movements aimed at the realization of some end. When human activity is characterized by these goal-directed motions, then that activity has become a Situation.

When actions are changed into Situations, the final machinery that produces ideal behavior has begun to operate. But the Situation still covers too many patterns of motion that are not. ideal. Many purposeful activities are mere matters of everyday planning which have little moral significance. Such Situations Hegel calls *Indeterminate Situations*.[9] Activity on these occasions contains purpose and organization, but our most important interests are not at stake. We plan a party or a game. These interests involve us in patterns of behavior that are goal-directed. But accomplishment of these goals is not of essential significance to us. Failure would frustrate but not destroy us. Therefore, the Indeterminate Situation can be regarded as a forerunner of the most significant situation, one in which our very sense of values is at stake, namely, the *Definite* or *Determinate Situation*.[10]

The Determinate Situation is the most crucial kind of activity in which men can be involved. Whereas in the Indeterminate Situation failure could be tolerated and even clearly considered as a possible outcome, such toleration and consideration would not be possible in the Determinate Situation. In the latter we are faced with the destruction of the most basic values. If we are not faced with death, then we are faced with the destruction of our very personalities. For this reason the Determinate Situation usually arises in social and psychological crises. Our very way of existing becomes threatened, and this, in turn, challenges the values and beliefs by which we justify what we are.

Even the Determinate Situation, however, might not exhibit the special ideal action which Hegel is trying to define. When we are menaced by some natural catastrophe—for example, an earthquake—we are able to do very little. Our lives are in danger, but at most we can only wait and hope. No real challenge exists which we can meet and possibly overcome and, therefore, no real demand for action is necessitated.

Hegel now calls to our attention the fact that every Determinate Situation has one essential characteristic, namely, *Collision,* or conflict.[11] In fact, only with the advent of collision can "the full seriousness and weighty import of a situation" begin.[12] But there are different kinds of collisions. As we have seen, one kind involves man and nature. It, however, is usually so completely determined that it affords little opportunity for men to engage in any counteractivities. There is still another kind of collision, which involves not a challenge between man and nature, but one between man and man. The collision among men is the immediate groundwork for the possible presentation of ideal action. Only as men clash with one another do their activities become conditioned by the need for intelligence, forethought, and moral resolution—the very factors which are displayed in ideal action.

Among these human collisions we can distinguish two classes. First of all, collisions occur in a social context. Individuals are in conflict with the social conventions of the time. The demand for conformity conflicts with the demand for individuality. The desire to change social conditions conflicts with the desire to keep the status quo. Such collisions, Hegel maintains, produce genuine human action. All the potentialities of reason and understanding are forced into actualization under the stress of events. In our everyday lives intelligence is primarily a mechanical concern with very undemanding problems. But in social conflict intelligence must be sharpened. We must call into play all those abilities which are normally not used. For this reason, ideal action first presents itself in the social collision. When a man is pitted against society, he is sometimes required to act in ways that are over and above the ordinary call of duty. He literally produces actions which have never been produced before and which become qualitatively different from any other forms of human behavior. They become the exemplars which men use to justify and construct their moral theories.

Social conflicts, therefore, are the immediate material in which ideal action can be displayed. And, as we shall see, Hegel argues that this is an important action which the artist seeks to describe in his work. The task of the artist is to use his particular medium to represent things and events as receptacles of ideal powers. The artist must have the genius to show the qualitative change that sometimes occurs in human action.

Although social conflict can be an exemplar of ideal action, it is still not the most important. More essential is psychological conflict.[13] The psychological conflict is not simply man's struggle against other men but man's struggle against himself. In the social conflict each side claims that it is right and the other wrong. When a resolution finally occurs, it is either a compromise or an application of force in which each side is still convinced that it is right. The resolution of the social conflict, therefore, does not usually produce some new form of belief and behavior which will make all parties happy. The ideal action here depends upon individual sacrifice and struggle, not upon any new synthesis of opposing forces. On the other hand, the psychological collision can never be resolved by compromise or force. The need for a new synthesis persists so long as the individual remains alive. The reason for this is that the psychological conflict is not the simple one of good versus evil. When we are involved in psychological difficulties we are aware of both good and bad elements in each of the opposing aspects of the conflict. For this reason, the synthesis that is demanded does not involve the acceptance of one part of the conflict and the rejection of the other. Once psychological struggle has begun, once doubt has been felt, the dialectic of thought forces us to search for some higher answer that will make compatible two apparently contradictory views. But moral conflicts of this sort cannot be resolved by any known moral principles. In spite of Kierkegaard's objection that Hegel was too much of a rationalist,[14] Hegel would have sympathized with the existentialist thesis that moral decisions are so-called leaps into the abyss. He recognized that genuine psychological conflict cannot be resolved by the acceptance of some specific standard set of moral principles.

Further, Hegel argued, such conflict is the only stimulus for man's endeavor to create more satisfactory moral syntheses. Only as men get into situations which challenge their most basic beliefs is it possible to obtain beliefs and values which lift us from the animal realm on to a more rational plane. Hegel would probably have disagreed with Nietzsche's contention that wars are the only means by which men are made better. But he would have agreed that social and psychological struggles have caused human advancement to evolve out of barbarism to at least an elementary stage of culture.

It is important to note that Hegel admitted that psychological problems often result in irrational rather than rational resolutions. But he was also aware that a synthesis of opposing psychological elements is not easily attained. Often people are unable to find a resolution and the conflict remains. But in some instances a genuine synthesis is found, and when this occurs the Determinate Situation becomes ideal. Man can then take a creative step forward.

With this analysis of action, Hegel can now fully state the

subject matter of artistic endeavor. Art seeks to depict the Idea. But since it cannot do this in conceptual form, it employs images and symbols. But what is to be imaged and symbolized? Hegel answers that the artist deals with those social and psychological conflicts that make up the Determinate Situation. These conflicts, which concern the most fundamental issues of life and death, right and wrong, good and bad, Hegel declares, are the supreme motive forces of art.

> They are the eternal religious and ethical modes of relationship, status, personal character, and in the world of romance, before everything else, honour and love. In the particular grade of their significance these powers differ, but all are essentially the product of reason. At the same time it is these powers in the human heart and mind, which man, by virtue of his humanity, is bound to recognize, to give free play to, and to actualize.[15]

Hegel's analysis, therefore, justifies artistic creation. And, furthermore, it serves as a device for classifying the arts in terms of significance. Art "is wholly restricted to the type of action which is conformable to the necessary configuration of the Idea."[16] Thus each art is to be evaluated by its capacity to describe the ideal action. As we shall see, Hegel examined each art in detail and concluded that the poetic art, which includes drama and literature, is the most important art form.

> The representation . . . of the action as a process complete in itself, in which action, reaction, and resolution are constituent elements, is, above all, the function of the poetic art; all the other arts can at most only seize upon and secure in their presentation one moment of this process.[17]

Hegel's analysis of action will be further examined when we consider his theory of the drama.[18] But several comments can be made at this point. First of all, Hegel maintains that the emphasis on the moral nature of the ideal action ought not to make us think that the actors involved in it are mere pawns. Even though the actors are exemplars of great moral forces, this should not be taken to mean that they have lost their individuality or their free will. All great actions are undertaken by men who have the freedom to act differently.

We can see this most obviously when we observe any great drama that deals with profound social and psychological crises. The hero is always one whom we can recognize first as a unique individual and second as a symbol of implicit moral powers. The hero cannot be regarded as an instance of the Idea in the same way we regard specific phenomena as instances of a scientific law. The variables in a scientific law can be replaced by any one of a number of different individuals of a given kind, but in the instance of the moral law depicted in the tragedy, one, and only one, hero is suitable. The hero does not merely convey a sense of righteousness. He embodies it so that the meaning of what is right can only be conveyed by recognizing and observing him.

We might best understand the kind of person Hegel wishes to describe by visualizing the heroes of Homer and the Greek tragedians. Achilles and Odysseus, especially, represent the living embodiment of universal ethical concepts. They are guided by gods (universal forces); they are not abstract symbols but men with their own unique personalities. Each of the Homeric characters—Odysseus, Diomedes, Ajax, Agamemnon, Hector, Andromache—Hegel insists, "is a whole, a world in itself, a complete and living member of humanity, something very different at least from your allegorical abstract of some one particular trait."[19] Thus the individuals concerned are not mere abstractions; they are not mechanical puppets.

First of all, even though they are capable of producing ideal actions, they do not have a full awareness of some specific set of moral principles on which they base their behavior. Odysseus is not a moralist. Secondly, Odysseus does not only symbolize Greek virtues, but he also seems to suggest an even greater moral synthesis than the Greeks experienced. If he is no more than an exemplification of some strict moral system, then this is a system that is still to be discovered. Odysseus, like an evasive puzzle whose answer always eludes us, can never be completely understood. For this reason the hero is always above the moral views of any given period. He represents the emergent product that will entail the revision of the old beliefs and the introduction of new ones.

A further comment ought also to be made concerning the relationship between social and psychological collisions. Even though we distinguish between the two types, both are usually found together. In every great social crisis one can find some individual or set of individuals who are involved not simply in the crises at hand but in the whole question of what is right and what is wrong, what is truth and what is falsehood, what is success and what is failure. When we read history we are fascinated more by the men who make history than by the events themselves. Analogously, the great artist is never satisfied with simply relating events. He insists on going further into the moral dilemmas in which his characters are involved. Sophocles does not merely tell a story of the misfortune of Oedipus, Eteocles, and Polyneices. He enters into the minds of the characters themselves and shows their inner struggles.[20]

He gradually leads us to recognize that behind every social crisis strange compelling forces are implicit in human thinking and behavior. Who can read Aeschylus, Sophocles, and Euripides, Hegel asks, without feeling that men are motivated by forces of which they themselves are unaware? Hamlet frightens us, Hegel notes, but he also fascinates us as we are frightened and fascinated by anyone who spends his life brooding and analyzing his own moral collisions. What holds our attention in *Macbeth* is the enigma of Macbeth's personality. We watch raptly as new energies and forces make their appearance. Odysseus is more of a hero than either Macbeth or Hamlet. But in both Macbeth and Hamlet we are brought into more direct contact with the source of power in living animals. Odysseus directs us to watch his actions; the Shakespearean characters direct us to watch the basic motivating source of all action. For this reason Hegel contends that Shakespeare was the greatest of all the dramatists.

Finally, the artist must be extremely sensitive to the medium he uses. For example, the great dramatist must not only know the denotation of words; he must also be fully aware of their connotations. One word incorrectly placed can destroy the meaning the author wishes to express. Ignorance of a shift in meaning can cause a profound idea to be changed into a commonplace. For this reason the artist must seek for maximum clarity. The idea he is seeking to communicate may be difficult to express, but this does not eliminate his responsibility for keeping ambiguity down to a minimum. Important art, Hegel declares, is never so abstract and abstruse that it would be meaningless to an intelligent audience. The meaning of a work of art ought not to be so obvious that no further investigation is needed. But at the same time it ought not be so hidden that no investigation can uncover it.

III. THE SYMBOLIC STAGE
OF ART: ARCHITECTURE

IN the last chapter it was pointed out that for Hegel the representation of ideal action and its underlying motives is the final aim of artistic endeavor. The arts can be classified consistently in terms of the aptitude an art has for giving this representation. Hegel concluded that poetry is best able to delineate the ideal impulse which sometimes permeates human behavior.

Hegel's analysis, however, leads to an even more significant conclusion. Since life is a process which gradually attains full realization in some men during some instances, and since, furthermore, process is the state of all beings, we should not be surprised to find that artistic endeavor also follows a cyclical sequence. Previously we described what Hegel believed an artist ought to do. But it would be a mistake to think that the knowledge of the artistic aim is given to men as soon as art begins. Such knowledge is dependent not only on the development of artistic techniques but also upon the state of learning at any given moment in history. Art, Hegel argues, develops as insight into the Idea develops.

At certain stages of growth one art form becomes more satisfactory than another in representing the Idea. Furthermore, each art form itself undergoes youth, maturity, and finally senility. Architecture, for example, passes through a series of transformations before it becomes all that it can become. The particular arts, Hegel states, have within themselves "a process, a progression, independently of the art-types to which they attach an objective reality, a process which in its more abstract relation is *common to all*."[1]

The production of a genuine art form is arduous and "implies a long series of experiment and practice."[2] When we refer to the beauty and simplicity of an art object, we are speaking about a result in which variety, medley, and confusion have been overcome, "so that at last Beauty, with all its unfettered spontaneity, appears to us as though liberated in one cast."[3] Therefore, it is not surprising that at the very beginning of art we find the appearance of clumsiness and artificiality. The most primitive products in all the various arts are essentially abstract, monotonous, confused, and stiff. The expressions on the faces are insipid, and the limbs of humans or animals are ill-proportioned. The very earliest types of poetry, Hegel declares, "are full of breaks, devoid of connection, monotonous, dominated in an abstract way by one idea or emotion, or elsewhere wild, violent, the particular being obscurely assimilated, and the whole as yet not bound together in a secure and ideal organic unity."[4] Gradually such deficiencies are eradicated, and the art production becomes a work of art in which "every expression, every modification . . . points to one thing only, and that is the idea and vital principle of the whole."[5] Thus the very earliest poetic writing is harsh and abrupt, whereas the epics of Homer as well as the sculpture of Phidias achieve the kind of organic unity that preceding artistic efforts lacked.[6]

Thus the artist is not over and above history. He also seeks for the right subject matter and the right medium. Like all other inquirers, the artistic inquirer struggles to find the proper way of expressing a conception that his age may only barely intuit. The Egyptian knew there was a Supreme Being. But he did not have sufficient knowledge of nature and man to know what this Being was like and how He manifested Himself. For this reason the Egyptian artist was limited. His description of this Being was vague and uncontrolled. The lack of reasoned information about divinity prevented him from finding a subject matter which would enable him to express himself. Hence his art was generally stiff and cold.

In relation to man's intellectual development, Hegel distinguishes three stages. In the first stage man begins to *wonder*.[7] Having finally struggled through to survival, man suddenly finds time to ask himself some startling questions. Who am I? What am I? What produced me? Why must I die? He recognizes that in spite of his affinities to the natural world, he is strangely divorced from it. For the first time "the facts of Nature astonish him; they become for him an other-than-himself he would fain appropriate, and within which he strives to [discover the kind of person he is and may become]."[8]

At this early period man is not at that stage of intelligence in which he "contemplates the entire external world as [something] which he has made himself clear about."[9] Nature is regarded as a power, but a power whose operations are un-unfathomable to him. As a result, man becomes obsessed with a desire to "render objective to himself his intuition of a higher, essential, and universal [Being], and to look upon its rehabilitated presence."[10] This desire produces the Age of Symbolism. Man now regards nature as a manifestation of some ultimate omnipotent power, and out of this view will arise the first endeavor at artistic expression—architecture.

The Symbolic Age, therefore, represents the initial stage of intellectual inquiry. The results are not very satisfying. At most, men have become aware of certain enigmas in experience. But the driving curiosity that permeates the Age of Symbolism leads to a new era which attains a more important insight into these enigmas. Gradually man gains a more proper perspective of the various strange events that occur in nature. The sense of fear and awe is replaced by the sense of confidence. The need for symbolic devices is gradually eliminated as men gain more information of the Being they seek to know. It becomes apparent that order exists in the world and that the primary cause for such order is some God or Gods which are all-powerful and all-knowing. Furthermore, the order prevailing in the world consists of a hierarchy whose apex is man. Hence man is the highest form of life and the most important creation of the powers resident in the universe. The study of mankind becomes primary for the new order, the Classical Age.

The new advance in knowledge has direct implication for the evolution of art. Art serves to make the abstract Idea at least partially concrete. Where, then, is the artist to find his subject matter in the Classical Age? For Hegel the answer is obvious. Since man becomes such a significant figure in this age, the artist turns to a study of man. But what kind of medium can best present man? In answer to this question the Classical artist develops a new art, sculpture. Whereas architecture was satisfactory so long as man sought for some symbolic version of the Idea, sculpture is more satisfactory in an age that feels assured it has a true representation of the Idea in mankind. This does not mean that architecture is suddenly forgotten. Architecture still evolves in its own way until every possibility of its being used as a symbolic device is exhausted. But in an age in which intellectual conceptions have changed, sculpture attains a more significant role.

Knowledge, however, is not stagnant. The Classical theory of the Absolute is not the final answer. The views of Plato and Aristotle are much more advanced than any of those expressed in the Symbolic Age. But Plato's Demiurge is at most a conception of a limited Deity. The forms, space, and time are restrictions rather than productions of the Demiurge. All the difficult questions dealing with the creation of being are left unanswered by Plato. Similarly, Aristotle's Unmoved Mover explains why things *move,* but not why things *are.* As these theological schemes are questioned, so also arise doubts about the adequacy of sculpture to represent divinity. A change in the conception of the Absolute results in a change in the conception of artistic expression.

The Classical view, therefore, in spite of its intellectual

achievements, has still not attained a satisfactory view of reality. A new change occurs which leads to the Romantic Age. For Hegel, the Romantic Age is the final synthesis in which the best of the Symbolic Age is combined with the best of the Classical Age. The Greeks believed that an examination of man's rationality is the key to an understanding of the universe. On the other hand, the medieval and Renaissance thinkers believed that the key was to be found in an examination of man's rational *and* emotional life. The Romantic Age, as Hegel labelled the medieval and Renaissance periods, also stressed man's rationality. But all those qualities which had been traditionally considered to be irrational, namely, feelings, attained a new and respected status. Both Plato and Aristotle discredited human passions. These emotional properties of mankind were best hidden while the search for the life of reason continued. But the Romantic Age made these very properties the marks of significance and uniqueness. Odysseus and Achilles were truly heroic figures. But essentially they were devoid of the emotional features that show true individuality. Primarily, they embodied ideals valued by the Greeks. On the other hand, Hamlet was an individual and not simply the expression of a type. In fact, the representation of highly individualistic characters became an important aim in Renaissance art.

The powers of nature, therefore, show themselves not only in those moments when man is acting in a purely rational way, but also when man is involved in anger, pain, frustration, desire, hate, fear, and love. Thus the classical emphasis on form and reason gives way to the romantic emphasis exemplified in the loving and often vengeful God of Christianity as well as in the introspectionism of a Descartes. Then, once knowledge of the Idea is seen to involve man's innermost thoughts and feelings, the art of sculpture is no longer satisfactory. Even though sculpture, like architecture, evolves to a high stage of development, it is incapable of presenting man as an emotional being. It cannot delve into the human mind in the same way as the new arts of the Romantic Age—music, painting, and poetry. These three are the highest art forms used to express the inner man. In these arts, especially poetry, we catch a glimpse of man as he is in his psychological rather than his physiological life. They show us the Idea as it reveals itself in man as a thinking and feeling being rather than man as a material object reacting in accordance with strict mechanical laws.

In outline, this is how, according to Hegel, art evolves. The next step is to make a detailed analysis of each stage. But before we turn to a more thorough investigation of the Symbolic stage of art, at least one critical point ought to be made about Hegel's concept of the evolution of art.

One standard objection has been raised by both art historians and philosophers. The fact that art undergoes change does not necessarily imply that the change is for the better. According to Hegel, the synthetic stage is always more advanced than the two prior stages that are being synthesized. For this reason the Romantic Age produces a kind of art that is more fully developed than any of the other arts. But, even if the notion of the Idea is acceptable, it is still possible to reverse Hegel's evolutionary theory of art. Sculpture, for example, may really be a more adequate expression of the Idea than painting. Even though sculpture does not use color as profusely as painting does, sculptors could and have used color creatively. In fact, even scenes including a number of figures have sometimes been utilized by the sculptor. Thus sculpture can give as adequate a representation of man as painting. Furthermore, sculpture need not use perspective and various other techniques in order to create a sense of depth. In sculpture the very shape and construction of the person himself can be depicted. For this reason painting might not be considered as adequate as sculpture in portraying ideal action and behavior. We could undoubtedly make a similar comparison of sculpture and architecture, or painting and architecture. In each instance it would be possible to draw the exact converse of Hegel's conclusion.

Of course, Hegel might have answered that painting actually does employ the techniques of color and scenery while sculpture does so only rarely. In fact, art critics usually depreciate the use of color and activity in sculpture, while these same devices are praiseworthy in painting. But it could still be argued that sculpture does *not* use these devices because they detract from rather than add to our insight into the human personality. By avoiding colors and the depiction of activity, attention is focused on the particular, unique person rather than on his behavior. On this analysis sculpture rather than painting would make for a more appropriate expression of the Idea.

Hegel's theory, therefore, is not without its difficulties. Nevertheless, such difficulties do not detract from the perceptive and seminal comments Hegel made about the specific arts. The drama may possibly not be more expressive of the Idea than painting or architecture, but this possibility does not detract from the significance of Hegel's discussion of dramatic action.

In his discussion of the Symbolic Age and the art form that it produces, Hegel first describes the development of the symbolic viewpoint. Nature becomes symbolic when man begins to wonder about its power. Objects suddenly attain a new status. They are regarded not as mere objects, but as signs of some concealed meaning. Nature taken as a whole is no longer a mere conglomeration of entities. It is now a covering hiding a more profound truth. In Hegel's terms, a symbol is "some form of external existence immediately presented to the senses, which, however, is not accepted for its own worth as it lies there in its immediacy, but for the wider and more general significance which it offers to our reflection."[11] But the arrival of symbolism in human experience does not indicate that men are aware of what is being signified by any given symbol. Hegel points out that something can be regarded as a symbol even though we do not know what is being signified. Each pattern of a Buddhist statue is considered symbolic and we may recognize it as symbolic even though we may be ignorant of what is being symbolized. When symbolism is first attributed to nature, philosophical and scientific analyses of natural phenomena are lacking. Men have no awareness of either the nature of the powers that create and destroy them or of the objects that would best serve as symbols of these powers. As a result, the earliest kinds of symbolism used by men, according to Hegel, are much too extreme. Either the object and its symbolic meaning are taken to be one and the same, in which case the very object is worshipped as a god, or else huge fantastic objects are created which express the first clumsy attempts at picturing the Absolute. The former kind of symbolism Hegel calls *Unconscious Symbolism,* the latter he calls *Fantastic Symbolism.*[12]

Unconscious Symbolism represents the first stage in the development of the Symbolic Age. The very earliest Oriental religions are good examples of this form of symbolism. In them we find a definite confusion of the symbol with the thing signified. In Zoroastrianism, Ormazd is sometimes taken to be the god symbolized by light and fire, but very often he is *identified* with light and fire.[13] Similarly, Ahriman is sometimes an evil god, but at other times he is both illness and evil. This kind of ambiguity permeates early religions. Even though nature is no longer regarded as a mere external entity, little understanding exists of the relation between symbol and significance. For this reason early Oriental art is of the most primitive order. These early artists do no more than imitate actual existent things. "The actual sun, stars, fire, organic nature, throughout its vegetation, animal and human life, [are] conceived as the appropriate form of the Absolute in this its existent and *immediate* shape."[14] But such work, according to Hegel, is hardly to be called significant art. No attempt is made either to bring in some profound idea or to produce a particular individualistic impression.

Gradually, there is an awakening to the fact that the symbol and the thing symbolized are two distinct entities. Hegel now proceeds to examine the growth of intellectual and, therefore, artistic insight into the distinction between symbol and significance. The insight is attained after a lengthy process. At first the artist only faintly intuits what a symbol is. He believes in a higher kind of reality than natural phenomena, but he does not know how natural phenomena are connected to this higher reality. Nor does he know what entities might best suggest the essence of this underlying divinity. As a result, it is not surprising to find the artist indulging in the most fanciful kind of symbolism. Lacking the awareness of what symbolism actually entails, the artist simply chooses as his model any existent object and then represents it in a highly distorted fashion. By such distortion he tries to portray the object as a vehicle for something other than itself.

During this period—the age of Fantastic Symbolism—the artist chooses any existent object without using any basic rationale and calls it a symbol of divinity. This stage of art is especially illustrated in the Hindu culture. The Hindu religion does not adequately define divinity. Its most important god, Brahma, is such an abstract being that his exact tie to this world is unknown. He is sometimes referred to as the Limitless One or as the One Thing, but rarely is a precise definition attempted. And since the theological conception sets no limit on the artistic imagination, the consequences are startling. "For the Hindu imagination the ape, the cow, and the particular Brahmin are not merely a cognate symbol of the Divine, but are contemplated and represented as the Godhead itself, as existences adequate to that Godhead."[15] Furthermore, the vagueness of definition leads to the most notorious exaggerations. One can find huge figures with many heads or many arms, swollen egg-like shapes designed to signify the world as a birth of Brahma. According to Hegel, the glorification of animals and bizarre statues derives from the fact that Hinduism never developed a clear theology. By not specifying satisfactory symbols it permitted anything to be an appropriate object for worship or artistic representation.

Both Unconscious and Fantastic Symbolism are preludes to the most highly developed stage of symbolism, namely, *Real* or *Genuine Symbolism*. This period arises when specific things or processes are finally designated as proper symbols for indicating divinity. When this stage is reached, the chaos of Unconscious and Fantastic Symbolism disappears. There is, of course, still ambiguity as to the nature of the Absolute. But at least it is clear that only certain entities can adequately be used as symbols. Thus men are now aware that divinity is characterized by permanence, power, and complete control over the process of living and dying. If symbolic devices are to be used, then these characteristics ought to be present. Thus the subject matter of art attains a greater precision than ever before.

The rule for the artist now is that he ought to deal only with objects which can be said to incorporate within themselves some features of the Absolute. This does not mean that such objects are *identified* with the Absolute. Hegel reiterates: "The form itself, this particular object, that is, whether in its glorified shape of grandiosity or in any other more conspicuous form of caricature, as an image of animal life, a human personification, event or action, is not taken to envisage for immediate sense an adequate existence of the Absolute."[16] Objects are to be chosen which *suggest* divinity. The question for art is this: Where is some model to be found which will best exemplify the features of divinity? What objects feature within themselves the characteristics of power, permanence, as well as the eternal process of living and dying? The artist finds his subject matter in architecture.

It is not too difficult to see why architecture becomes the most significant form of symbolic art. Architecture most obviously incorporates in itself some of the properties that are attributed to divinity, namely, power and permanence. Furthermore, as it evolves, architecture turns out more and more to be a habitation for beings which live and die in it. Therefore, to the symbolic artist architecture seems to be a perfect symbol for representing the Idea. It becomes the primary medium for glorifying the existence of the Absolute.

Hegel does not believe that architecture suddenly springs into existence. The advent of Genuine Symbolism is gradual. Similarly, the advent of the architecture that will finally satisfy the needs of Genuine Symbolism is gradual. The first constructions had little architectural significance. Primarily utilitarian, these early mud huts or tents served as a means of physical protection. However, as men became more inquisitive about nature and its powers, as they sought ways and means of propitiating these powers, these same constructions began to attain more than a strictly pragmatic function. Furthermore, since such physical protection was sought even for the dead, the construction that housed the dead became identified with the mysterious and the occult. In time the propitiation of the gods became the task of the chieftain of the tribe and his house became the temple of the gods. Once architecture was divorced from strictly practical needs, its use as a religious symbol became a primary concern of artistic endeavor. In its first phase this new attitude toward architecture was expressed in the creation of great image-producing edifices. The very construction itself was designed to stimulate some imagery of a higher reality. Herodotus stated that the Chaldeans erected huge temples which consisted of seven floors and an eighth highly ornate floor, representing the seven planets and the home of the gods. In India the same attempt at image production was seen in the construction of huge stone columns which broadened out at the base. The phallic symbolism was quite obvious. The memnons and obelisks of India and Egypt were designed to play a similar role. They were huge constructions whose purpose was to convey a definite image of some higher sanctified being. The Sphinx was probably the best example of the use of architecture to present a picture. By making this unique combination of man and lion, the artist was able to secure an image of some vast rational power which could never be destroyed.

The attempt to employ architecture in this way does not last very long. Once buildings and constructions are regarded as artistic subject matter, it rapidly becomes apparent that the purpose of architecture is to build *enclosures* rather than glorified sculptures. For this reason there develops a new type of architecture which incorporates two functions. On the one hand, the old image-producing function is still present. But, on the other hand, the building is now also conceived of as a container for some internal mysterious significance.

Hegel points out, for instance, that this dualism is quite evident in the caves of Mithras in Persia. These caves are arranged so as to be a replica of the observed arrangement of the stars, yet they also serve as enclosures for the dead.[17] This dual purpose, according to Hegel, also serves to explain the Egyptian pyramids. The primary purpose has already become the one of enclosure of the dead. For this reason the structure as a whole is no longer one huge portrait. But the image-producing effect is still present. Originally the pyramids were covered by a casing of highly polished slabs of stone which glittered when the sun's rays struck them. This effect served to produce an image of a great shining power, a good symbol of the sun-god, Re.

The pyramids were important, Hegel points out, not only because they signified a transition point but also because they brought an important emphasis into architecture, namely, the emphasis on mathematical precision. The slabs of rock used in constructing the pyramids were cut to very precise dimensions. The corridors and passages within the pyramids were ingeniously planned to contain the tremendous pressures that were present on all sides. From this time on, mathematics was to play an important role in the evolution of architecture.

As Oriental architecture evolves there is a gradual disappearance of the appeal to imagery. Even though the temples are covered with numerous ornaments and surrounded by huge figures, the basic structure itself becomes primarily an enclosure, a protection, for some hidden inner meaning. The structure of the pyramids is subordinate to some symbolic meaning; that is, the shape of the pyramids is due to the need to produce some symbolic impression. But the prime purpose of later architecture is to be strong enough to serve as a protection. This does not mean that architecture becomes strictly practical. The medieval cathedral, Hegel will argue, has in itself tremendous symbolic significance. But such significance is clearly secondary to the main aim of giving adequate protection to some internal objects which are more genuine representatives of divinity.

Once architecture is defined as an enclosure for some more meaningful object, artistic interest then turns toward this meaningful object with the aim of expressing it in some artistic medium. Out of this new interest will eventually arise a new form of art—sculpture. But the change in artistic focus does not thereupon relegate architecture to an unimportant status. On the contrary, even though the function of architecture is primarily that of an enclosure, the problems of finding a satisfactory means of enclosure always remain to be solved. Thus architecture moves from a stage in which symbolic devices overrule any other considerations to a stage in which the basic need to create strong and useful dwellings is of paramount importance. We should not think, however, that this new change eliminates the need for aesthetic effect. Symmetry, proportion, and aesthetic appeal are still required. A building must not be so constructed that it seems to trivialize or vulgarize its objects of divinity. The architecture that appears in the Greek Age—the Classical Age—best combines pragmatic functionalism with aesthetic dignity.

For Hegel, the Greek Age was an admirable one. It exuded confidence, knowledge, and trust in man's rational faculties.

It was an age in which men took a huge step forward in answering the questions of who they were and why they existed. The Greeks of that era apparently excelled in almost everything. Their philosophy, drama, and sculpture attained excellence. Even though the great art of the Classical Age was sculpture, the other arts, such as architecture and the drama, fulfilled potentialities that had never been realized before. Thus the mathematical precision that the Egyptians were beginning to require in their work was now rigorously employed. The endeavor to make architectural works into enlarged bits of sculpture was forgotten.

Constructions were now built with a view to their scientific soundness and their capacity to lend dignity to the valued objects that were housed in them. As a result, knowledge of mathematical and physical principles became standard equipment for the creating architect. Curved lines were replaced by straight lines for the simple reason that mathematics was more applicable to straight lines. Early architecture was often characterized by naturalness. That is to say, there was a deliberate attempt to make constructions appear to be outgrowths of nature. But the Greek Age rejected this conception on the ground that man's reason was stronger than nature. Thus buildings were to be made of lines, squares, and precise proportions so that mathematics, the highest result of man's reason, could be utilized.

We should not think, however, that mathematical precision is the sole influence in Greek architecture. Buildings also reflect the importance of the affairs that are carried on within them. If men are to worship the gods, then they ought to do so in buildings which enhance rather than detract from the feeling of sanctity that is meant to permeate the interior. Hence the Greek architect made another addition to the requirement of mathematical precision. He insisted that buildings be pervaded by the quality of aesthetic unity. His creations were to be perfect fusions of the science of mathematics and the art of aesthetics. Thus, the columns of the Parthenon are deliberately tapered in order to give an impression of elasticity and life and to avoid the stiffness which would have resulted if strict mathematical precision had prevailed. Similarly, the columns along the sides of the Parthenon incline inwards not because the mathematics requires such an inclination but because the desire for organic unity is satisfied in this way. When the Greeks observed the Parthenon, Hegel argues, they must have received a sense of what is befitting and appropriate to the high values that were present on the inside of this great work. Aesthetic effect had to be combined with a high degree of mathematical precision.

Hegel is aware that not all Greek architecture exhibits the splendor and perfection characteristic of most of the work done in the fifth century B.C. The Basilica of Paestum, built in the sixth century B.C., has none of the grace to be found in the architecture of the next century. Much of the Egyptian stiffness and heaviness is to be found in the construction of the columns. But this fact, Hegel maintains, does not detract from the general perfection of Greek architecture in its golden age.

Hegel used a wealth of detail in order to elaborate his views on the aesthetic quality of Greek architecture. He made a very close inspection of the Doric, Ionic, and Corinthian columns and differentiated the aesthetic from the strictly technical reasons which caused changes in style. Hegel was so certain of the skill and success of Greek architecture that he was unable to believe that even the smallest deviation from mathematical exactness could have been due to error. On the contrary, he firmly maintained that such changes were deliberately created in order to produce an aesthetic effect in the mind of an observer. Hegel would undoubtedly have rejected later views that the settling of the Parthenon caused the warping and inclination of the columns, or that the Greek architects really desired straight lines and believed they would obtain them when the building settled.

For Hegel, the architecture of the Greeks was a reflection

of an intellectual attitude that was sensitive to the need to bring beauty into human experience. The Egyptians made no such demand. They required mystery rather than clarification, awe rather than satisfaction. The Greeks had attained the stage of knowing and wanting enriched experience. The Parthenon was not simply a symbol of some hidden meaning. It also produced an immediate experience of pride and aesthetic satisfaction.

The Greek culture was indeed a marvellous advance over all preceding cultures. But as the deficiencies of the Platonic-Aristotelian scheme of reality became apparent, as Greek society eventually destroyed itself through internal dissensions, man's confidence and feeling of certainty began to evaporate. As philosophical speculation proceeded to indicate the problems in defining the Form of the Good and the Unmoved Mover, so also artistic interest began to lose the quality of clarity and inspiration. This change in intellectual viewpoint was not only to affect the development of architecture, but was also to entail major changes in the most significant classical art, namely, sculpture.

The change in artistic viewpoint was clearly seen in Roman architecture. Since there no longer existed a scheme of reality that clearly defined the gods and their relations to man, the Romans did not expect their architecture to produce an effect of unity, simplicity, and clarity. The pantheism of the Stoics and the hedonism of the Epicureans made men more conscious of mundane than of celestial values. Thus the Romans regarded architecture as a science for designing buildings which were essentially for the comfort of men. Unlike the Greeks, the Romans looked for utility and the sense of power in their buildings. For this reason some of the most impressive Roman works were of an entirely utilitarian nature, as, for example, the aqueducts and the elaborate private homes. The Pantheon is a good example of the Roman desire to experience power and massiveness in their perceptions of great architecture. This does not mean that the Romans were insensitive to aesthetic needs. But whereas for the Greeks the aesthetic element was a necessary characteristic of their constructions, for the Romans this characteristic was merely incidental. Consequently, the Romans sought only the superficial accouterments for aesthetic effect. In the Arch of Titus, for example, the function of the columns is decorative. They no longer operate as supports. Similarly, in the Colosseum the columns are descriptive rather than structural in function.

Even though the Romans no longer required the same degree of aesthetic satisfaction as the Greeks, they did advance the purely scientific aspect of architecture. The need to create powerful effects made them investigate the kind of walls and ceilings which would best support very heavy structures. Thus they developed and perfected the arch and the vault constructions.

With the Romans there was a dearth of aesthetic feeling. The kind of spiritual uplift that the Greeks expected in their art was not expected by the Romans. Roman art, therefore, was essentially specious and imitative. A new outlook was required which would again give back to architecture its essentially artistic character. This new outlook originated in the age of Christianity—the Romantic Age.

With the arrival of the Romantic stage of art, architecture evolved to its highest point. Even though painting, music, and poetry were far superior to architecture in giving men an experience of divinity, Christianity was an inspiration for every art. The Christian architect combined symbolism and classical rationalism in order to produce a work that inspired awe as well as aesthetic satisfaction.

Hegel traces in great detail the full development of medieval architecture. He points out that the very earliest church buildings display little spiritual quality. This, of course, is understandable in view of the fact that first and foremost the early Christians needed buildings in which to conduct services. Thus many of the early churches, such as Old St. Peter's in Rome, incorporated numerous pagan concepts. The early

Christian basilica form of structure relied heavily on features found in the Roman basilica and house. Practical considerations, at least in the early period, were more influential than spiritual desires.

Gradually, however, the demand for a purely Christian type of architecture made itself felt. The Christian builder eventually felt it incumbent upon himself to make his work not only technically sound but also spiritually symbolic and in order to achieve this he made special use of the concept of space. One of the most important aspects of Deity for the Christian is His infinity and immateriality. He is everywhere and in everything, yet He is not material.

What the architect sought, therefore, was some means of molding matter so that the effect of infinity and immateriality would be reflected in both the interior and the exterior of the church. Some of the very early attempts to obtain this effect consisted in the introduction of pieces of colored glass plastered into the walls. The resulting glow aided in creating an atmosphere that seemed to suit the abstract semi-mystical thought of Christianity.

Similarly, the failure of the medieval architect to solve the problem of the construction of windows in the massive walls of the church served to add to the general mood of solemnity and piety. Columns in the interior were deliberately spaced in order to focus attention on the apse as, for example, at Santa Sabina in Rome. As Hegel put it, the impression that art had now to emphasize was "in one aspect of it, and in contrast to the open gaiety of the Greek temple, that of the tranquility of the soul which, released from external nature and worldly conditions, retires wholly into self-seclusion; in the other aspect of it it is that impress of a solemn sublimity, which strains and soars over and beyond all rational limits."[18]

However, by far the most important element in the creation of the atmosphere of infinity and immateriality consisted in the changes in the spatial perspective of the church. The medieval architect found that the sense of vastness and of infinity could be produced by means other than those employed by the Indian and the Egyptian. The use of various shapes, such as spires and buttresses on the exterior as well as vaulting and domes on the interior, could produce a tremendous feeling of awe and sublimity in a spectator. Thus the erection of appropriate domes and vaults was one of the major problems for the medieval builder. Hegel examined in detail the various difficulties that beset the builder in his endeavor to develop these constructions. He discussed the partial successes of the Byzantine and Romanesque architects. But his major analysis centered around the high point of medieval culture, the twelfth and thirteenth centuries, when the Gothic style finally gave Christianity a distinctive architecture.

In the Gothic period the problem of giving the impression of great height was finally solved. Several important innovations provided the solution. First of all, the use of a groined vault with pointed arches served to add immeasurably to the effect of height. Whereas the Romanesque arch was usually semicircular and therefore lacked the vertical apex which gave the Gothic arch a sense of elevation, the new arch, by being pointed, made the interior of the church seem to be boundless. The pointed arch as well as the pier also caused the eye to move upwards instead of horizontally. Secondly, the use of the flying buttresses solved the problem of obtaining adequate window space. Huge, thin sheets of glass could now be inserted into the walls. As a result, many different lighting effects could be obtained in the interior which had never been seen before. Thirdly, the Gothic cathedral stressed vertical features wherever possible. Thus the cathedrals at both Amiens and Chartres clearly convey, in both their interior and exterior, the impression of enormous space. The pointed form of the windows, the spires, the towers, and the buttresses with their gables and pinnacles all contribute to the impression of great heights reaching into infinity. Even the ornamentation, which one might think would keep interest attached to one area, serves to raise the mind into infinite heights. As Hegel puts it:

On the one hand we cannot fail to observe the most obvious outlines in a clearly defined co-ordination, on the other we have full-
ness and variety of delicate embellishment impossible to follow
with the eye, so that the most motley particularity is directly set
up in contrast to what is most universal and simple, just as the
soul, in the opposition implied in Christian worship, is deeply
engaged in finite things, and indeed carries its life into the mere
detail and the trifle. This very opposition acts as a stimulus to
contemplation, this striving up invites to a like action.[19]

The particularity of the ornamentation and the largeness and
spaciousness of the building itself produce a contrast that sym-
bolizes the very essence of Christian faith.

Hegel's discussion of Christian architecture is, of course,
much more extended and detailed than is suggested here. The
main point of this meticulous and exhaustive investigation
is that Christian architecture fulfills a need that is felt by the
more profound mind. In Hegel's view, only one who has an
awareness of the philosophical advances of Christian over
Greek thought can truly appreciate Gothic architecture. The
Greeks sought symmetry and balance in the works they wished
to experience. These factors were sufficient to produce an
aesthetic experience. But a mind that has become aware of the
difficulties in the Greek scheme of reality can no longer be
satisfied with the stability and rationality that permeate Greek
art. To the Christian, only God is perfect; only He is completely rational. Furthermore, man is not actually what the Greeks
imagined him to be. The Greek ideal of man was a pure
rational being cleansed of passions and desires. But the Christian ideal depicted man as a struggling, suffering individual
whose passions were as much a part of himself as his rational
and material self. Gothic architecture appealed to the Christian
because it represented the striving upward, the driving force
in man that made him look for a higher truth than that given
by the Greek rationalists.

Hegel believes that Gothic architecture is the highest phase
of development for architecture as an art form. It signifies
symbolism at its very best. Avoiding the excesses of uncon-

scious and fantastic symbolism, the Gothic style constantly directs one's mind to a higher reality. The knowledge of mathematical and scientific techniques serves to temper this symbolism and imbue it with a restraint and dignity heretofore unattained.

The Gothic stage, however, shows also the limitations of architecture as an art form. With all its greatness, architecture can never be as important for art as the contents which it encloses. Nor can its forms ever have the same profound meaning for men as sculpture or painting. The latter, unlike the former, can give us a direct insight into living beings themselves. Architecture can at most suggest life and power. Painting can show us divinity expressed in living organisms. Architecture can only express divinity as an abstract intangible Being. For this reason the greatness of the Gothic style cannot overcome the basic shortcomings in architecture as an art form.

We should not think, however, that the deficiencies of architecture become evident only in the Middle Ages. During the era of the Egyptians it was already clear that architecture was inherently incapable of ever giving a completely satisfactory representation of the significance it sought to symbolize. Thus, for example, the Judaic conception of God as a powerful and sublime figure is incapable of being symbolized by architectural works. In fact, the Jews expressly prohibited the use of material forms as a means of giving artistic expression to their view of Deity, and employed writing as the best means for celebrating their God.

Similarly, the pantheism inherent in many early Oriental religions could not be symbolized by architecture. The pantheistic view of divinity does not imply the existence of one particular entity responsible for the creation of all other beings. On the contrary, pantheism identifies God as a composite of all existent entities. His being is exhausted in the infinite number of entities in the universe. But such a conception cannot be revealed in architecture or, for that matter, in any single existent entity. Only poetry is able to suggest such meaning, since of all the arts poetry alone is able to extend its meaning into infinite directions. Painting alludes to one or a series of finite entities; it cannot specifically present the connections among objects.

Unlike poetry, which can use words whose meanings explicitly refer to the divinity of all objects, painting is restricted to the presentation of concrete entities. Thus the pantheism of the Orient, especially in India and Persia, is given a poetic art form. The *Bhagavad-Gita* and the Mohammedan *Oschelaleddin-Rumi* are examples of the use of poetry to express pantheistic views. Only in literature can the artist bring forth "that joyful ardour of the soul, that liberal happiness, that revel of bliss, which is so peculiar to the Oriental, who in freeing himself from his own particularity seems wholly to sink himself in the Eternal and Absolute, and henceforth to know and feel the image and presence of the Divine in all things."[20]

Judaism and pantheism reveal the limitations of architecture as an artistic form at a very early stage in history. These two religious views contain conceptions which are incapable of being exemplified in physical constructions. For this reason they foreshadow the rise of new art forms which can more adequately indicate divinity. Unfortunately, the orientation of the times was not sufficient to develop the great artistic potentialities latent in poetry. So long as divinity is regarded as an abstract Being whose relation to man is not defined, poetry as an art form remains in a minor stage of evolution. Writing was indeed used to depict Judaic and pantheistic ideas. But this use of language did not long continue. Instead, the writer turned his mind to ideas which could more easily be understood. Poetry, therefore, at this early stage was employed either to signify some definite moral belief or to show the cleverness of the writer in the use of words. Artistic interest was directed towards concrete and pragmatic rather than religious issues. Out of such interests developed the Fable, the Riddle, and the Allegory. In this kind of writing "we have nothing more than a quite ordinary course of everyday occurrences, from the isolated reproduction of which we are able to abstract in a way commonly intelligible an ethical *dictum,* a warning, example, or rule of prudence, by whatever name we choose to call it, which is set before us in a form that appeals to our imagination for the sake of the reflections it carries with it."[21]

Poetry that is primarily didactic or concerned simply with clever techniques is, for Hegel, furthest removed from genuine art.[22] Such writing does no more than attempt to communicate very obvious information in a witty and artificial style. There is no attempt to show men something ideal and inspirational. There is no fusion of form and meaning such as we find in Homer or any of the great tragedians. When the form is incidental to the meaning, art itself disappears since it loses its reason for being; when the meaning is incidental to the form, art loses its importance since meaning has been trivialized. An age that can give the poet a genuine theory of the Absolute will finally bring poetry to its highest fruition. But before this age is reached the dissatisfaction with architecture will lead to an attempt to utilize a new art—sculpture.

IV. THE CLASSICAL STAGE
OF ART: SCULPTURE

THE age of symbolism is the first stage of man's intellectual development. Knowledge at this stage is primarily allegorical and irrational. For this reason the first art to develop is that which deals with large and massive bodies. These are the objects that, to the symbolic mind, could best exhibit the features of divinity. But man advances. Knowledge increases. The symbolic outlook toward nature gradually disappears as philosophy changes from a simple imaginative study into a complex conceptual inquiry. Because they lacked a fully developed philosophy the Hindus and the Egyptians were unable to give their artists a subject matter that was clear and distinct.

During the Greek Era, philosophy attained an unparalleled significance. In that age the Absolute was definable in terms of a strict set of gods who were primarily concerned with the affairs of men and who in appearance and intellect were similar to men.[1] Thus in the Greek period the artist had a more advanced knowledge of how best to represent divinity. Neither massiveness nor mere physical impressiveness were to be the prime subject matters of artistic inquiry. The study and depiction of man himself was to be the genuine substance of artistic interest, since, as Hegel phrases it, the human form is "alone capable of revealing the spiritual in sensuous guise."[2] The human body is not merely a material receptacle. It is something which itself incorporates the activities of the Abso-lute.[3] The Greeks assumed a hierarchy of being in which the highest form—so far as man is able to perceive it—is man him-self. In man is to be found the true combination of universal Spirit and concrete object. In him is to be found that fusion of significance and form which the symbolists sought but could not find. The very body of man is a strange material in which there is not merely a combination of parts. On the contrary, the parts are fused together in a way uniquely different from any combination found among inanimate objects. The human body is very similar to the animal body, but the Greek philos-ophers, such as Plato and Aristotle, believed that the potenti-alities of spirit are most fully actualized in the human being. Man alone, because of his particular kind of matter and shape, can bring to perfection the qualities which lower forms of life either lack or incorporate in only the most primitive fash-ion.[4] For these reasons the Classical stage of art deals primarily with the human form. Living things become the focus for ar-tistic endeavor. Thus the most important art form is sculpture, for this art can best present human shapes.

The concern with human form involves the artist in more than mere imitation of the kind of bodies observed. The human figure reacts to a great deal that is strictly mechanical or biological. Circumstances, various illnesses, and psychologi-cal disturbances frequently annihilate the uniqueness of man and lower him to the animal level. It is the function of art "to expunge the divergence between the purely natural and the spiritual, to exalt the external bodily appearance to a form of beauty, that is, a form throughout dominated and suffused with the animation of spirit."[5] Not man per se forms the content of artistic subject matter, but, on the contrary, man as he can and ought to be.

The classical artist, therefore, no longer has the problem that prevailed during the Symbolic Age. The search for enti-ties which correctly designate the Idea is no longer a crucial one. The artist has finally attained an image which contains

a final fusion of entity and significance. This image is an outcome of the new intellectual advance in the artist's culture.
Where originally the intellectual forces of a culture struggled
to make the definition of the Idea a complete one, the new
intellectual era regards the definition as finally complete.
Thought has now emerged to a greater clarity and no longer
accepts a purely symbolic conception of the creative force in
the world. Of course, the Classical Age has still not fully
explicated the nature of the Absolute. The recognition that
conflicting ethical and emotional crises best reveal the most
essential element of the Absolute is not present in the Greek
period. The ideal of Greek art is essentially one of undisturbed
harmony.[6] But philosophical inquiry has finally extricated
itself from the vagueness of Oriental speculation, and history
is now marked by an air of clarity and certainty. The trouble-
some search of the Symbolic Age has vanished, and the Absolute is presented to the classical artist "as something *already
there* in the sense that as a thing essentially positive, as belief,
popular opinion, or as an actual event either of myth or tradition, it is determined for his imagination in all its essential
character."[7] Thus, the Greek artists received their subject
matter from a religion whose gods and goddesses were already
fully determinate figures. Phidias, for example, was able to
borrow his conception of Zeus from Homer, and the tragedians also were able to utilize religious images that had been
clearly defined.[8]

Like symbolic art, classical art also is a developing processs.
Art, like any other intelligible subject matter, is not characterized by sudden abrupt transitions. Classical art, therefore,
undergoes various phases from its first differentiation from
symbolic art to its final disintegration into romantic art.

During the Symbolic stage various natural entities were
given a divine status. Animals as well as mountains were considered to be symbols of divinity and, therefore, themselves
divine. Even the ancient Hebrews, whose God was over and
above nature, retained at least a vestige of worship for natural

objects. Thus Moses forbade the use of animal blood as food because life is centered in the blood.[9] However, man's survival rests on his use of nature for his own purposes. Accordingly, as man's needs increased, animal and nature worship began to deteriorate, as when the early Greeks ceased to worship living animals but rather the sacrifice of animals. The animal itself became a gift to an acknowledged Deity. And as the Greek culture advanced animal worship declined still further. The slaying of certain animals became a mark of courage and heroism. The wolf, for example, which for the Egyptian was a friend of the gods, was for the Greek an enemy. In the *Metamorphoses* of Ovid, Lycaon's conversion into the form of a wolf is regarded as a punishment for his impiety.[10] For other various misdemeanors Cygnus became a swan, Daphne a laurel, Narcissus a flower, and Biblis a flowing spring. The change of men into animals or other forms of nature was regarded as a misfortune and a humiliation.

Man's conception of nature was thus transformed. For the early Greeks divinity came to man by means of various natural phenomena. The rustle and whisper of the oak, the murmurs of the spring, the sound of the wind—these were all instruments by which the message of divinity was to be conveyed to the mind of man. But gradually these instruments lost their extranatural meaning.[11] Not nature, but man, in the guise of the oracle, became the best vehicle for the commands of the Absolute. Hence it is not difficult to understand how, gradually, the Greeks began to regard the Absolute as a Being with human form. The Titans, the very earliest Greek gods, were essentially like animals in that they lacked human emotions and desires, but they already had the form of human beings. Prometheus, Hegel points out, was not very far from the animal level since he "was unable to furnish mankind with anything . . . spiritual or ethical,"[12] but he was still represented in the shape of a man.

Once the Absolute was given human form, it was not long before men invested it with characteristics not only of a natural but also of a spiritual kind. As Greek culture developed, Zeus became a power of nature. But he also developed into the thunderer and "as with Homer already thunder is the sign of misfortune or assistance, is, in short, an omen, and as such is relative to that which is human and spiritual."[13] Similarly, the early conception of Aphrodite depicted her as a force of nature; but "once arrived in Greece, the spiritual and more individual aspect of her grace, charm, and love [and] passion is more emphasized, albeit here, too, the natural basis is by no means entirely absent."[14] In this weakening and gradual disappearance of the natural factor in the presentation of the gods, the Greeks accomplished what the Symbolic Age could not. They created a conception of divinity that was concrete and yet divorced from the inanimate and animate world. The conception of divinity was fused with the material that could best reveal it, namely, the human body.

It is important to recognize that the Greek artist, like prior artists, also obtained his conception of the universal significance from the type of culture in which he lived. The Homeric gods, for example, "are not to be taken as the result merely of the poetic phantasy, or nothing more than capricious invention. They have their roots in the genius and beliefs of the Greek folk and the religious basis of that nation."[15] Since Greek culture regarded the gods as having human traits, the Greek artist was not concerned with mere nature nor with symbolic entities that designated some abstract being. Rather his subject matter was derived from human existence and therefore pertained to everything that was valuable to man.[16] But the artist presented only those aspects of human existence which designated godly actions and divine powers.[17] For this reason the Greek artist was more of a creator than the Oriental artist and required many more talents. Not only did he have to be capable of eliminating actions, events, and aspects of the human condition that were insignificant, but, like the priest and seer, he had also to be able to discern how divine powers were interfused with human action.[18] In short, the

Greek artist had to know the kind of human actions and attributes which gave men godlike qualities. The question, therefore, arose: What are those actions and attributes which give
godliness to the human form?

First of all, the being who is to personify a god must be
represented as more than merely mortal. He must not be
depicted as one afflicted by human ills and suffering. Unlike
human beings, the god must not be constantly influenced by
external conditions. He is a permanent being, ageless in body
and in personality. Adversity does not affect him, and he never
undergoes the human emotions of desperation, fear, and
hatred. This does not mean that he is a bare, abstract ideal who
does not partake of situations and activities. On the contrary,
the god is an individual and concrete being similar in many
respects to ordinary human beings. But he is never impaired
by age and, more important, whereas the human being is not
compelled by natural law to act ethically, the god, in spite of
his frequent eccentricities and purely human foibles, is controlled by "a definite natural force, with which a definite ethical consistency is blended, such as imposes on every particular
god distinct bounds to the sphere of his activity."[19] Thus Zeus
signifies the might of the state with all its rules and regulations; Apollo is the god of prophecy; Hera celebrates the ethical bond of marriage; Athene represents moderation and good
sense.[20] Each god, by his very nature, is required to act in accordance with specific ethical rules.

A second characteristic of the Greek god concerns his physical figure. Since the emphasis in representing the gods is on
the spiritual rather than on the natural, the physical form
must be purified of those ills that befall man because of his
ties to nature. All defects must be erased; the lines and shapes
in the human physique that draw attention to man's kinship
with the animal world must be minimized if not completely
eliminated. Such features as the chin, the eye, and the nose,
which are most capable of conveying character, must be han-
dled carefully and delicately because these features are highly

capable of revealing the spiritual aspects of the human body.[21] Even the hair must be treated in a certain way.[22]

Therefore, the concepts that will become important for the Greek artist are clearly delineated by the religious views of his time. All that is needed is some medium in which these concepts can be expressed in a sensuous form. Sculpture becomes an art that satisfies this need.

Sculpture, as an art form, originated out of a desire to enhance the appearance of architecture. Thus the earliest sculpture functioned as adornments of tombs and temples. However, the recognition that architecture could never really be more than an enclosure did a great deal to stimulate interest in sculpture for its own sake. But, according to Hegel, sculpture can never actually be divorced from architecture. Although the statue appears to operate as a single unity exclusive of the environment in which it is placed, "a statue, or a group, and yet more a relief, cannot be made without considering the place in which such a work of art is to be situated."[23] One should not first complete a sculptured work, then consider where it is to be placed. Rather "it should in the very conception of it be associated with a definite exterior world, and its spatial form and local position."[24] Hegel argues strongly that the best sculptured figures are those which are displayed "apart from all situation, in beautiful, unimpaired, and inactive tranquillity, or at least free, unmolested, without definite action and development."[25] However this type of effect is attained only by incorporating the sculptured figure into an environment which permits the realization of freedom and tranquillity. Thus, architectural works, such as churches and temples, are the most appropriate places for really great works of sculpture.

The problem of discovering a satisfactory environment for sculpture is, however, not the crucial one for the sculptor. The prime concern is the discovery of an adequate subject matter. Hegel believed that for the Greek artist this problem was solved. The unique human bodily figure is the prime subject matter for sculptural activity, since it, rather than the animal body, is most capable of revealing the Idea. Hegel reiterated his contention that human consciousness more completely expresses itself in the human body than animal consciousness expresses itself in the animal body. Spirit, Hegel declared, more completely permeates human than animal flesh.[26] Human beings have actualized what is only potential in the animal.

However, sculpture cannot reproduce all the characteristics of human beings. Unlike painting and other romantic arts, it cannot portray the emotional life with all the various psychological complexities that human beings undergo. For this reason great sculpture avoids too much concern with capturing human emotions. Its primary concern should be "with *form* and *nothing more.*"[27] The sculptor is unable to utilize the painter's ability to use colors and the poet's ability to use images in order to convey a variety of traits and feelings.[28] This does not mean that there are no examples of painted sculpture. The Egyptian idols are of painted wood. The Zeus of Phidias is colored, and many other Greek carvings exhibit ivory and gold ornamentations. But, Hegel declared, such paintings and ornamentations detract from the work as a whole. In most instances they are merely concessions to "vital popular necessities,"[29] just as the stage setting of a Greek drama is modernized in order to catch the popular eye. But such appeals are not intrinsic either to great sculpture or to great drama.

The fact that sculpture cannot adequately represent emotions and actions does not imply that sculpture gives us only abstractions or "types." On the contrary, every work represents a particular individual, but the individuality is obtained by emphasizing permanent rather than accidental or momentary traits in the human personality. In order to clarify this distinction, Hegel defined two basic kinds of personality. One type constantly shifts and changes as conditions shift and change. Such a personality never attains self-reliance and is "dependent upon particular circumstances as they happen to arise, and is unable generally to dispense with this association with something else."[30] When the individual is so dependent, he is indeed a "product of his environment." He does not exhibit any real permanent traits. On the other hand, the second type of personality attains a self-awareness of the impact of conditions and can, therefore, react to some extent against environmental conditions by retaining a unique individuality. Such individuals retain consistent integrated personalities despite adversities of all kinds.

The traits that identify such integration are the ones the sculptor seeks to represent. Sculpture seeks to portray the permanent core of man, that genuine personality of man which is to be found when all artificial and accidental features have been removed. In a biography, for example, we are told how a given individual reacted under various conditions: numerous incidents, events, and exploits are listed. But at the end of this account is a character sketch which outlines those general qualities that this particular individual has always exhibited. Qualities such as these, Hegel declared, "we may term the permanent features of a personality; the remaining peculiarities it possesses are merely accidental features in the impersonation. It is just this stable aspect of life which it is the part of sculpture to present as the unique being and determinate substance of individuality."[31] The best sculptor, Hegel continued, always studies and portrays individuals, but he portrays them "as essentially complete and enclosed within their objective spiritual presence, in their self-subsistent repose, delivered thereby from all antagonism as against external objects."[32]

Human beings are usually "preoccupied, in their demeanor and expression of face, with themselves, their dress and attire, in general terms, that is, their purely personal particularity, or, at least, matters of momentary importance, and any unforeseen or accidental features thus presented."[33] But changes of such a kind, as well as the momentary smiles or outbursts of anger, must be ignored. "Sculpture must rather concentrate its attention on the permanent traits of spiritual expression, and retain and disclose such in the posture and configuration of the body no less than in the face."[34]

Sculpture, therefore, is properly involved in inquiring into the nature of the human figure. Like other arts, however, sculpture is not merely imitative. It imitates, but at the same time it eliminates the accidental and searches for the ideal, which is not at the mercy of conditions that cause deterioration and illness in the human body. Such ideal figures are not attained by the production of perfect physical figures, but by the combination of physical perfection with permanent intellectual expression. The sculptor has the important task of creating in his medium the perfect fusion of mind and matter.

Hegel was aware that the search for such perfection takes time and patience. Like architecture, sculpture evolves from a state in which sculptured work is still obscure and uncertain to a stage in which all the potentialities of the art are fully realized. This stage of completion occurs in the Greek period. In this period sculpture attains its highest peak, even though numerous works incorporate various symbolic and romantic features. This art actualizes what architecture by its very nature never could. Architecture, no matter how far it advances, is necessarily symbolic, since it can never reach a point in which there is complete fusion of the symbol and what is signified. On the other hand, this fusion does occur in sculpture. The meaning is no longer external to the object. We shall see also that sculpture attempts to incorporate various romantic features such as those found in the Laocoön group and various medieval sculptures. However, Hegel regards this as a mistake. Sculpture by its very nature is unable to incorporate those features that can be best represented in the genuine romantic arts, such as painting, music, and poetry. The inner emotions of the human personality can only be suggested by the sculpture; they do not undergo the kind of intensive scrutiny to which the romantic arts subject them.

The first beginnings of sculpture are to be found in Egypt. And, as in all the arts, the earliest phases are the most amateurish. Even though there are occasional instances of independent artistry in Egyptian culture, most of the work was designed primarily to be used as an ornamentation for the houses of the dead. Hegel believed that this purpose served to restrict the artist. Instead of bringing in his own feelings and reactions, the artist sought to carve figures and scenes that represented the occupant of the tomb engaged in some heroic activity. Thus, carved scenes show the king observing the headless bodies of his enemies or in the act of slaying an enemy. Little attempt is made to reconstruct these scenes so that the artist's own talents are revealed. Since Egyptian culture is essentially mechanical and formalized, the figures are created in accordance with rigid conventions governing the proper representation of kings and nobles. The artist is a mere craftsman "working in a purely mechanical and abstract way according to forms and rules ready at hand, rather than with the vision of his own . . . unique creation."[35] In agreement with J. J. Winckelmann, whose *Geschichte der Kunst des Altertums*[36] was extremely influential in forming Hegel's judgments on art, Hegel found Egyptian sculpture to be crude and immature. "The outlines are straight or in lines that show [little deviation], the pose appears constrained and stiff, the feet are thrust close together, and in cases of figures in the upright position where one foot is placed before the other, both point in the same direction instead of having the toes turned outwards. In the same way, in masculine figures, the arms hang down straight and glued to the body."[37] In short, Hegel observed, "so far as detail is concerned, despite the laborious and able execution, just that aspect of the elaboration is absent which alone communicates to the figure its true animation and vitality."[38] Even in the few instances where an attempt is made at realism and animation, as, for example, in the "Sheikh-el-Beled," the wooden figure in the Cairo Museum, there is the same rigidity and lack of expression. Egyptian art was never able to realize the potentialities implicit in sculpture as an art form. Full realization came only with the efforts of the Greeks.

As in architecture, so in sculpture, the Greeks gave a tremendous impetus to artistic effort. The reflective, inquisitive, and freethinking minds of the Greeks brought life and color into all their artistic adventures. The Egyptian was unable to break the shackles of convention; the Greeks broke them and went on to create "the consummate plastic union of divine and human."[39] Obviously, Hegel was fond of Greek sculpture. It is therefore understandable that he lavished special praise upon Winckelmann and Lord Elgin.[40] Their efforts succeeded in revitalizing interest in Greek art and civilization.[41]

Hegel was very specific about the reasons for his great admiration. First of all, the general features of Greek sculpture made it excellent and gave it a gracefulness and suppleness that created an immediate feeling of form perfected to its highest degree. The rigidity of Egyptian sculpture is no longer present. The straight lines have given way to more natural flowing, curving lines that give the sense of life and restrained movement. The Doryphoros, for example, shows superior mastery of the balance and harmony of the human figure, There is a rhythm that permeates the sculpture and creates a feeling of poise, confidence, and restrained power.

Hegel also made specific comments about Greek sculpture. He believed the carving of the face to be a genuinely remarkable achievement. Each facial characteristic was the result of an inquiry into the question of what form of face would tone down man's animality and emphasize his rationality. The nose, for example, was not merely an artistic convention that the sculptor employed mechanically. It was deliberately designed in such a way that all purely animal features were placed in the background. The nose was to be regarded as a unit in a symmetrical whole rather than as an entity designed to fulfill some bodily need. "The Greek profile must in fact not be regarded as any mere external and accidental form, but approximates to the ideal of beauty by its independent claims, namely, . . . because it is the type of countenance in which the expression of soul-life forces into the background all that is purely material."[42]

The forehead also is employed to enhance the spiritual effect of the face as a whole. The Greeks believed that a wide forehead, a feature not found among animals, was a sign of wisdom and virtue. Thus there is a correlation between the shape of the forehead used in sculptures and the intellectual prowess that is signified. Usually the gods and great heroes are shown with wide foreheads; lesser individuals have narrower foreheads. Hercules is somewhat of an exception since his forehead is quite small. But Hegel believed that the reason for this is that "Hercules possesses rather the muscular vigour of the body directed towards external objects than the introspective energy of mind."[43]

The eye, at least insofar as its external features are concerned, is adequately and naturalistically represented in the Greek statue. Except for a few simple effects, such as the deepening of the interior, the eye is incapable of adding much to the spiritual quality of the whole. A careful molding of the eye can do a great deal to convey a sense of introspection and profundity. But those emotional and soulful qualities that the eyes are able to express can be produced only in the romantic arts, especially in painting. Hegel thought that the attempt sometimes made to paint eyes into the marble or bronze sockets was unsuccessful. The medium of sculpture makes the appearance of color and ornamentation seem very garish and out of place.

The Greeks also made a very important study of the mouth. The very best work should portray the mouth slightly open without the teeth showing. This appearance is appropriate, since the mouth "when . . . we are absorbed in visionless thought . . . opens slightly and the angles of the mouth are to an appreciable extent inclined downwards."[44]

The chin was required to be full and round, since these characteristics convey the impression of repose combined with strength. Withered chins, or chins that are sharply etched, ought to be avoided since they lead to an emphasis on the purely physical and also give the impression of "old fussy wenches"[45] wagging and bickering.

The standing position also was a Greek device for adding to the general spiritual effect. The reason for this is that "as soon as consciousness begins to awaken, man wrests himself from the animal chains of the earth, and stands straight in free independence."[46] Picturing men as sitting, lying, or crawling is too suggestive of animal postures. They suggest an attitude of "subordination, dependence, and serfdom."[47]

In spite of his admiration for Greek sculpture, Hegel did not approve of nudity in sculptures. His reasons were ingenious. After all, he declared:

> It is the sense of modesty which compels man to cover himself with raiment. Now, this shame, regarded in a general way, is a beginning of indignation over that which is coarse and crude. Man, in fact, who is conscious of his more elevated calling to be Spirit, must necessarily regard what is purely animal as an incompatibility with that, and pre-eminently seek to cover, as that which is not consonant with the Ideal of his soul, those parts of his body, such as the belly, breast, back, and legs, which are subservient to animal functions, or only are directed to external uses, and possess directly no spiritual determinacy, and no spiritual expression.[48]

It is true that the Greek statues are frequently nude. However, the nudity is generally found in youths, children, wrestlers, fauns, satyrs, and other lesser spiritual beings. Cupid, for example, is shown undraped because he represents youthful innocence. Nudity is also found where the emphasis is on the physical, as in the bodies of Perseus, Hercules, Theseus, and Jason. On the other hand, where the sculptor is dealing with the highest spiritual values of the human being, he places drapery over the intimate parts. Thus Pallas, Juno, Vesta, Diana, Ceres, and the Muses, whose earnestness and dignity are emphasized, are draped.[49]

All these features, Hegel believed, were carefully examined and thought out by the Greek artist. Every facial expression, every human mannerism, was studied and modified in accordance with the over-all plan of exhibiting the perfection of the human form. We should not think, however, that the Greek artist sacrificed individuality for perfection. Hegel insisted that Greek sculpture combines both perfection of form as well as uniqueness; the sense of omnipotent power is fused with personality. The Hermes of Praxiteles, for example, is not simply perfectly formed; its individuality makes us think of this figure as a model of a being that could have lived. Similarly, the creator of the figure of Theseus on the Parthenon shows a profound knowledge of the human body as well as a sensitivity to the need to create individual rather than typical beings. The curving of the lips and the shaping of the nose signify the use of special devices in order to produce individuality. Phidias' Zeus also attains his uniqueness by virtue of the unusually solemn expression given to his face and of the special care taken with the styling of the hair. The large circular arched eyes and the use of a particular hair style make Polycleitos' Hera proud, commanding, and unforgettable. The less arched downcast eyes of the Pallas on the Parthenon give the impression of "more austere maidenhood and chastity."[50] Finally, Praxiteles' Aphrodite obtains her inimitable sensuous and yearning look by the precise and subtle molding of the eye. "Her eye, even in cases where a more grave and lofty expression is emphasized, is smaller than that of Pallas and Juno, not so much in length, but narrower by reason of the lower eyelid being slightly raised, by which means Love's yearning look is admirably expressed."[51]

Another method for producing individuality comes from the expressiveness of the body itself. The Greek sculptor uses lines and etching in order to convey impressions of youth or old age. When the lines are softer and more curvaceous, we obtain the impression of youth. To signify more mature figures the lines are cut more deeply and with more emphasis. In the bodies of the Laocoön group, Hegel notes, soft and sharp lines are used to convey the image of youth and maturity respectively. Muscles are also ways of indicating age.[52] The muscles of youth are smoother and less sharply defined than those of old age. But, Hegel points out, the Greek sculptor had to be very careful when he shaped muscles. If the muscles of the youthful Apollo, for example, had been too well-rounded he would have appeared flabby and flaccid.[53]

Finally, the sculptor sometimes resorts to the use of external objects in order to give identity to his sculpture. Thus, Zeus is often accompanied by the eagle, Juno by the peacock, and Venus by the hare. Such identification, however, is not too effective since the gods are often identified by the same object. The vase is frequently associated with Jupiter, although it is also found with Apollo, Mercury, Aesculapius, Ceres, and Hygeia. The lily is found in the hands of Juno, Venus, and Hope. Even lightning is not the exclusive property of Zeus—Pallas has it also.

Sculpture was the highest form of art that the Greeks used in order to express their view of reality. Since they were committed to the principles of reason and observation, sculpture became for them the primary art. The tremendous number of Greek sculptures—indeed, thousands were to be found in individual cities such as Elis, Athens, and Corinth—is explained by the Greek's need to visualize his gods.

> A more spiritual religion can rest satisfied with the contemplation and devotion of the soul, so that works of sculpture pass for it simply as so much luxury and superfluity. A religion so dependent on the sense of vision as the Greek was must necessarily continue to create, inasmuch as for it this artistic production and invention is itself a religious activity and satisfaction, and for the people the sight of such works is not merely so much sight-seeing, but is part of their religion and soul-life.[54]

Although Greek sculpture is indeed one of man's greatest attempts to envision and give concrete form to divinity, there are still, according to Hegel, fundamental deficiencies in sculpture and in the religious view that makes sculpture so significant. Even at its highest peak a basic difficulty is discernible in Greek art and religion. On the one hand, the human body is regarded as the perfect receptacle for the expression of universal divinity. On the other hand, the nature of the god is such that his tremendous powers make it almost inconceivable that a single body can be sufficient for him to accomplish all that is required of him. The personality of the god seems to be too strong for a human body, even if that body is considered perfect. In the final analysis the body is a limitation; some activities are not allowable precisely because the body is constructed in the way that it is. But the notion of such limitations tends to damage the image of omnipotence that is attached to the gods.

Recognizing this contradiction between the infinite spirit and the finite body, the Greek artist tried to endow sculpture with melancholic characteristics. The silent, serene expression that marks the best of Greek sculpture is not completely analogous to human expression. Rather it is the feature that signifies a truly free spirit enclosed in a finite domain.[55] The aloofness sometimes said to characterize the Greek gods is not due to their arrogance, but to the universality that the gods possess, to their disinterested concern with temporal affairs.[56] They can never undergo the kind of satisfaction experienced by human beings. Whereas for human beings satisfaction occurs when particular finite problems are overcome, for the gods satisfaction comes from looking "far away and over death, the grave, loss and temporality."[57] It is precisely because Greek religion implicitly recognized the difficulty of correlating a divine force with a finite body that the artist brings the expression of melancholia into his work. Perfected beauty, Hegel declared, is not satisfied with being tied to a particular specific existence. It demands freedom from the restriction necessarily imposed on spirit by a particular type of body.[58] As Socrates had pointed out, the truly wise man recognizes that his material shape is no more than a handicap to his spiritual substance.

Thus, in spite of the perfection of form in Greek sculpture, in spite of the fact that the Greeks discovered the best receptacle for expressing divinity, the very restriction to space and time is a limitation to the spirituality that is attributed to the gods. Even though sculpture is, for Hegel, "the highest and most adequate form of representation for the classic gods,"[59] there is still a sense of enclosure. The gods, in their repose, give concrete expression to the profundity and mystery that resides in the Absolute, but because of their limited bodily characteristics they cannot exhibit all the dynamic features that are usually attached to godhood.

As a result of these limitations two consequences follow. First of all, sculpture loses its place as the highest art form. The feeling grows that as an art medium sculpture is inherently incapable of doing full justice to divinity. Secondly, in a final attempt to indicate the action and energy that the gods signify, sculpture becomes humanized. Whereas originally the divine personalities were characterized by complete repose, now they appear "within the variety of the individual and external embodiment, in all the detail of events, occurrences, and actions, which become ever and ever more human."[60] The gods are "made to blend in a vital way with human affairs."[61] Gradually they become identified with human actions of strength, courage, and so forth. Thus the Medicean Venus and the Belvedere Apollo, even though essentially serene, begin to suggest possible actions. Apollo is caught in the very act of letting fly an arrow. A more imposing kind of animation occurs when group sculptures are initiated. The famous group of Niobe and her children is an excellent example. But the best example is the Laocoön group, which was executed about 50 B.C.

Hegel felt that the entire discussion which Lessing had provoked was not very meaningful. In agreement with Winckelmann he insisted that sculpture could not and ought not to try to express emotions. The fact that Homer often represented the gods as giving vent to their emotions did not imply that such emotional behavior was proper in sculpture. In fact, Hegel thought this lack of restraint a fault in Homer. Homer makes Ares shriek with pain when he feels the lance of Diomedes. Both Apollo and Ares are emotionally as well as physically involved in the Trojan War. All such representations of the gods detract from the ideal image that ought to persist. Strong emotion, therefore, was properly purged from sculpture in general and from the Laocoön in particular.[62]

But Hegel does not judge the Laocoön group to be a great work. The figures are adorned too elaborately; mannerism has become too important. In fact, the humanization found in the Laocoön signifies the eventual deterioration of Greek sculpture. The concern with the human situation rather than with divinity points to a new approach to art which will now depict the gods as essentially finite and undergoing finite pleasures and activities. Art becomes amusing and "the seriousness of the gods becomes a grace, which does not agitate with violence or lift a man over his ordinary existence, but suffers him to persist there tranquil, and simply claims to bring him content[ment]."[63]

Roman culture completes the dissolution of classical sculpture. The Romans are no longer capable of appreciating the full import of the Greek ideal. As a result, in Roman sculpture "it is no longer upon the true Ideal that the entire conception and execution depends."[64] There is now an insistence on realistic imitation, and the art of Rome is characterized by a preference for portraiture studies. Hegel admired the portrait sculpture of the Romans, but the Romans could never capture the idealism and spirituality of the Greeks.

It would seem as if sculpture could have a rejuvenation in the new spiritual concepts of Christianity. However, this does not actually happen, since the new modes of thinking are best embodied in other arts.

Pain, torture of body and soul, martyrdom and penance, death and resurrection, the personality of the individual soul, inner life, love, and emotional life in general—this characteristic content of the romantic imagination, in a religious sense, is no object, for which the external form, taken simply for what it is in its spatial entirety, and the material which belongs to it in its more sensuous existence unrelated to ideality, can supply either a form that is wholly relevant to it, or [a material] similarly congruent with it.[65]

The main role of sculpture in Christian art is one of embellishment for architecture. Where sculpture attempts to incorporate romantic concepts, it usually is forced to violate classical principles and, therefore, is a confused effort.[66] Hegel admits, however, that a noted exception to this statement is the art of Michelangelo, who was able to combine successfully a romantic imagination with a sense of classical form.

Even when dealing with religious subjects the genius, the power of imagination, the force, thoroughness, boldness, in short all the extraordinary resources of this master tended, in the characteristic production of his art, to combine the plastic principle of the ancients with the type of intimate soul-life which we find in romantic art.[67]

Christian emotion, however, does not lend itself to the creation of the kind of work produced by Michelangelo. Sculpture is more concerned with external characteristics than with the introspective and emotional qualities significant to the Christian Age. For this reason, other modes of art must "infallibly arise able to reach in very truth the mark which sculpture failed in its work to achieve."[68] These new modes signify the rise of the romantic arts.

V. THE ROMANTIC
STAGE OF ART

THROUGHOUT the Symbolic and Classical stages of art the primary task of the artist was to give concrete form to the unique force in experience. As the nature of this force received a more adequate definition, art became better qualified to realize its highest potentialities. Out of the fumblings and ambiguities that prevailed in symbolic art, an art developed that finally discovered its most suitable subject matter. Hegel considered the Classical stage a perfection of the Symbolic stage. What the symbolic artist endeavored to accomplish in his work became a realized fact in classical art.

However, intellectual inquiry into the nature of the Absolute was not stagnant, and gradually the deficiencies of the Greek conception became apparent. Even the Greeks themselves became aware of the inconsistencies of their religious views. Thus, both Socrates and Plato lashed out against the superficiality and anthropomorphism of the Greek religion, and Aristophanes began to ridicule abstract conceptions. Such challenges did not go unnoticed by the Greeks, and later the satires of the Roman artists completed the debasement of the classical ideal. The satirical works of Horace, Sallust, Livy, Tacitus, Juvenal, and Lucian testify to what occurs when art perceives "this breach between the abstract conceptions of the inward life and the objective world around."[1]

The ideals of the Greek culture were no longer intellectually

85

satisfying. The Idea may not have been adequately presented in the Symbolic stage, but this inadequacy appeared in the Classical stage as well. The gods had become too human and too finite to give a sufficient representation of that unique force that men felt permeated the universe. How could omnipotent beings be immoral, vengeful, and perverse, as the Homeric gods are sometimes represented? How could it be that gods are frequently afflicted with human weaknesses? The Greek ideal was no longer satisfactory. A new approach to the Idea was required.

Only gradually did philosophy reach another level of analysis. The gods of the Greeks became transformed into the God of Christianity. Philosophic speculation attained the important insight that God is to be found by self-examination, not by the fruitless search for some external entity which occupies Mount Olympus. Anselm and Augustine argued that men who search their own minds and examine their own ideas will really find the meaning and significance of divinity. Descartes also insisted that simply through the examination of our own ideas and feelings we could prove the existence of God. Suddenly, with the arrival of Christianity, especially the medieval and Renaissance periods, the inner man (the famous ghost in the machine) became the most important source of information of divinity. Man's reason and emotions became manifestations of an underlying force which sought to express itself in matter. The medieval and Renaissance thinkers spoke of these powers as aspects of soul. Kant called them powers of an inherently unknowable substance. Fichte called them surges from a hidden unfathomable Ego. But all these thinkers were convinced that if anything at all was ever to be discovered about the Absolute it had to come through an intensive examination of man's mental and emotional life.

This new insight gives the artist a new clue in depicting the Idea. Divinity can no longer be exhibited simply in human form. Winckelmann, Hegel argued, was only partially correct when he said that the highest beauty is embodied in the human figure. True beauty resides in the human spirit. As Plato had long ago pointed out, genuine beauty refers to a thing's essence and not to its matter. Artistic endeavor, therefore, is to be directed toward those properties which best reveal man's essence, namely, his intellectual and emotional responses. The artist has to be trained both in describing objective phenomena and in indicating subjective motivations and reactions.

Hegel noted that this new concern with man's emotional and intellectual characteristics does not reduce art to a mere subjective process. Utilizing differentiations that had been introduced by Kant, Hegel attempted to make a bifurcation between the subjective and universal nature of spiritual conflicts. Art does not deal with the momentary frustrations and pains of everyday living. On the contrary, the subject matter of art concerns those problems which all men endure, The fear of death, the desire for love, the relation of finite being to infinite being—these are all matters which men universally encounter and seek to resolve.

Man, Hegel stated, in seeking self-knowledge is involved in the most agonizing of conflicts. The creative ideal part in him is in constant struggle with the irrational brute element.[2] The new task facing the artist is to examine and present to mankind the Idea as it is revealed in man's spiritual struggles. The romantic artist, unlike the classical artist, does not concentrate upon the human physique. He deals with such physical attributes only insofar as they suggest internal struggle of some highly significant import. He studies men as they live their lives and in the course of which "arise both strain and conflict, and the appearance and reappearance, as an essential feature of it, of pain, death, the mournful sense of non-reality, the agony of the soul and its bodily tenement."[3]

The romantic artist has a great advantage over his predecessors. Earlier artists, in spite of their reliance on religious sources, had to supply their own images. Thus the Greek gods, no matter how much they are humanized, are essentially products of imagination. They never look or act like genuine existential beings. On the other hand, Christianity introduces a concrete particular Being as an embodiment of God Himself.

> It is Christianity which first introduces us to this reality in flesh and blood as the determinate existence, life, and activity of God Himself. . . . In a word, God is acknowledged as present in the actual world. This new content, then, is not brought home to consciousness by means of the conceptions of art, but is presented from an exterior source as an actual occurrence, as the history of the God who became flesh.[4]

Thus, the romantic artist has a fully developed religion which he can use for his inspiration. Furthermore, the romantic artist can give an even greater concreteness to the concept of divinity because Christianity emphasizes the divinity of individual men rather than the type, or kind, which is so important for the classicist.

Not essence alone, but each individual substance partakes of divinity. The Christian conception of individual man as God and God as individual man implies the fact that "the human spirit *intrinsically*, that is, relatively to its notion and essence, is Spirit in truth; and every particular individual in virtue of the humanity he connotes possesses the infinite vocation no less than the infinite significance of being an object of God and in union with God."[5] This conception of divinity gives the artist an interest in the particular individual for his own sake. Human beings, with all their flaws and errors, become the proper subject matter for the romantic artist.

The immediate consequence of this new definition of the nature of the Absolute is an interest in those features and traits of human beings which will convey the impression of profundity and understanding. But these characteristics must not be abstracted and used to suggest a type. They must be embedded in all that is finite and concrete.[6] For example, Hegel declared, in Christian theology Christ represents man generally, but this does not mean that he is to be depicted as an abstraction. Some painters do present Christ as a classic ideal. All human flaws are erased. But Hegel regards this as a mistake.

> Such heads or figures of Christ may no doubt display earnestness, repose, and ethical worth: but the true Christ presentment should rather possess on the one hand soul-intensity and pre-eminently spirituality in its *widest* comprehension, on the other, intimate personality and *individual* distinction.[7]

Hegel was aware that it is an extremely difficult task to combine individuality with universality. First of all, there is the problem of discovering those facial expressions which can become symbols to men of psychological suffering and divine wisdom. How, specifically, are the purely Christian traits to be painted into a face? Can the face of a Socrates be used to signify the divinity of Christ?

A second task deals with the kind of individuality needed. The romantic artist is committed to delineating concrete figures. But how concrete are they to be? Christ must be represented as human. But if He becomes too human His divinity suddenly disappears. We shall see later—specifically when Hegel examines painting—that these questions plague the romantic artist. But in the attempt to answer them the romantic artist produced some of the greatest art works men have ever created.

Not only Christ Himself, but also the various incidents and events relating to His history, become subjects for artistic treatment. The story of the Passion, the suffering on the Cross, the Calvary of Spirit, the agony of death—all of these occurrences are suitable as artistic subjects. They challenge the artist to show the universal in the particular. But the Christian conception which pleases the artist most, which makes the greatest demands on his talents, concerns the most fundamental relation between man and divinity—the emotional experience of love.

For Hegel, the fact that man has the ability to love is the highest form of evidence for the presence of divinity in human-

ity. Love, Hegel maintained, is a unique phenomenon in that
it is the only feeling which is directed toward the welfare of
another. Love "consists in the surrender of the self-consciousness, in the forgetting oneself in another self."[8] Whereas all
other human feelings may be thought of as directed primarily
toward the well-being of the self, love deals with the well-
being of another. Even though the emotion of love involves
self-satisfaction and physical attraction, these elements do not
sufficiently account for the love relationship.

We love when we intuit in another the existence of a kind of
compassion and understanding that destroys our fears and
motivates us to fulfill our potentialities simply to satisfy the
other. Love ties us to another in a way that nothing else can.
But this tie only serves to make us fully sensitive to what we
can and ought to do. We may object to the fact that we have
to drink water in order to survive. But at the same time we
must recognize that this dependence causes us to grow and
develop in a way that would not otherwise be possible. Love
operates in a similar manner. It stimulates men to look for
potentialities which they can and ought to actualize primarily
for the sake of the happiness they will produce in another.

This emphasis on love is, for Hegel, one of the most significant features of Christianity. It signifies an intellectual awareness of the strangeness of at least one emotion that is present in
all men. Hate, fear, frustration, desire, and anxiety may all
be due to strict physiological causes and may serve to protect
the physical organism. But love is the sole emotion that makes
men altruistic and selfless.

The attempt to describe love and to present it in an artistic
medium is an extremely difficult task for the romantic artist.
At least in painting the artist must be able to show an internal
emotion solely by use of external properties, and this is no
easy matter. However, Hegel was convinced that there is a
"bond of affiliation"[9] between an inner emotion and an external appearance. The feeling of love makes its appearance
"through the bodily members themselves, through a look, the

facial expression, or in a still more spiritual way through the voice tones or a word."[10]

Hegel was aware that it would be difficult to uphold the view that there is a causal connection between an emotion and its physical expression. Too many examples can be given of the way in which the same emotion gives rise to different physical expressions. However, Hegel believed that in every culture some physical features are taken to signify certain sacred qualities, such as wisdom or foresight. The criterion for asserting a connection between emotion and expression is not logical in the sense that there is a necessary connection between them. The criterion is derived from the various religious and traditional beliefs that are handed down. Thus the physical representation of the Christ figure is modified as each age changes and recasts its explication of the kind of divine qualities attributed to Christ and the kind of external features which best exemplify these qualities.

The artist accepts the data of tradition and religion. But he is still required to bring his genius to bear on the organization and proper casting of conventional symbols. The use of certain lines in a face will give age and maturity to that face, but, of course, not in all instances. If the nose is not correctly sketched, if the eyes are not properly drawn, then the use of lines will not serve the purpose of the artist. He alone is responsible for using his medium in such a way that possible hindrances to the effective transmission of a profound idea are eliminated.

The expansion of Christianity gives the artist numerous subjects and events which he can use. But, Hegel points out, some aspects of Christianity are rejected as suitable subject matter for artistic treatment. The greatness of Christianity lies in its purity and humility, not in its excesses. Thus the artist usually rejects dealing with self-renunciation and martyrdom since these occurrences are for the most part no more than fanatical abuses which can be so extreme that they must "lie much too remote from beauty for any sane art to think of selecting them for its subject-matter."[11] We may be fascinated by the techniques that an artist employs in depicting horrible scenes. But such scenes, because of the revulsion they effect, will never be able to yield "a harmonious work of art."[12] Furthermore, in any work that involves physical torture or strenuous physical activity, there is always the danger that emphasis on the physical situation may trivialize its spiritual significance. Generally, Hegel repudiated any sort of fanaticism and asserted that the mind of the fanatic "both in its self-inflicted sufferings and its renunciations, is from the rational point of view simply mad, so mad that we can neither feel any profound compassion for it, nor propose any means of liberation."[13]

The artist, therefore, ought to deal with the spiritually elevating elements of Christianity. And, indeed, the most significant painting shows Christianity in its purest form. But the artistic endeavor to express the finest of Christian idealism changes as Christianity becomes a political as well as a spiritual power. Once the Christian faith has secured a firm foothold in the world, it becomes more and more institutionalized. In its endeavor to procure membership and leadership in communal affairs, Christianity is forced to become more mundane and thus to relinquish its hostile attitude towards things of this world.[14]

The new religion of Christianity becomes transformed into a way of life that can be satisfactorily practiced in a world community. As a result something begins to happen to early Christian values, which are more concerned with the city of God than the city of man. The love expounded by the early Christians was more preoccupied with God than with any earthly entity. Even ordinary human love was taken to be genuine only if it was a result of spiritual rather than physical attraction. Similarly, the early Christian made faith in God more important than faith in any human leader. For this reason stress on individuality and on the sanctity of the person was very important. But this belief did not lead to pure egoism. Each man was responsible for knowing his own divinity, but he was also responsible for knowing and appreciating the divinity of others.

Such beliefs, however, are vitiated when Christianity is victorious and the Christian becomes a symbol of militant righteousness. The early values change into values that incorporate social and political connotations. Thus, in the medieval period the fundamental Christian ethics are transformed into honor, love, and fidelity. Unfortunately, these ethical beliefs are by no means identical with the original ones adhered to by the early Christians. Honor in the medieval period is an egoistic term. It makes any insult to the person a crime against individuality. But such a view makes a man more interested in himself than in God. Honor, Hegel argued, does not refer to one's integrity or to one's obligations to his God. "On the contrary it contends simply for the recognition and formal inviolability of the individual person."[15] It is a perversion of the original Christian belief that men ought to respect and seek to understand all personalities, not for their own sake but for the sake of insight into the divine reality. The medieval conception of honor was to respect personality for its own sake. Honor "has no reference to the factual values of real things, property, status, obligation, etc., but to personality simply, and its idea of its own importance."[16]

This extreme stress on the importance of honor is unique to the medieval period. Not even the Greeks were ever really aware of such a conception as honor. It is sometimes argued that Achilles' feeling of anger against Agamemnon because of the division of booty involves a feeling of honor. But Hegel denies this. Achilles' feeling, in Hegel's reading of the *Iliad,* is primarily due to his belief that he had not received all the material goods to which he was entitled. The insult is not based, as it would have been if honor were involved, on any feeling that he is an individual whose personality must be respected. A primary part of the ritual of appeasing Achilles is the return of the abducted slave and the addition of other goods and bounties. But the medieval hero obviously would never have been mollified by mere material compensation. The idea that personality itself must be respected was external to the Greek conception of justice.

Hegel would undoubtedly have agreed with Berdyaev and other contemporary existentialists that the sanctity of personality is one of the most significant Christian beliefs.[17] But he was aware that too much emphasis on the individual could lead to an exaggerated feeling of self-importance and, finally, could produce the view that each man is a law unto himself. The medieval man of honor was apparently led to this conclusion. Thus the man of honor does not concern himself with the essential rightness or wrongness of any action, but "whether it is the right thing for him to do, whether it becomes him then as a man of honour to make himself master in it and to stand by it."[18] A man can be a man of honor and still perpetrate "the worst actions."[19] Sometimes an individual creates an idealized image of himself which is unlike what he really is. When this image is challenged, the individual feels that his honor has been violated. It is natural that such consequences should occur for "honor is the extreme embodiment of *vulnerability*."[20] The greater the importance an individual attributes to himself, the greater the possibility that he will encounter threatening situations. The smallest offense can be designated as a personal attack. Thus honor so exaggerates the notion of man's independence that no end of struggle and contention is incurred. If honor has any value, it is only that it at least calls attention to man as an important spiritual entity. It is a "positive consciousness of his infinite [worth] independent of the content."[21]

Thus, situations in which honor is an intrinsic constituent become, along with the purely religious events, an important source of material for the romantic artist. In spite of its frequently pejorative connotation honor is still a psychological phenomenon, and the artist is now primarily concerned with the psychology of human beings.

Just as the medieval conception of honor is a perversion of

a pure Christian value, so also the medieval conception of love is a perversion of the love that was expressed by the early Christians. Divine love, unlike romantic love, is primarily altruistic. But this is only partially true of romantic love, which requires that the object of love be completely enslaved. Furthermore, the stimulus toward self-realization, an accompaniment of genuine or divine love, is less significant in romantic love. Genuine love is always combined with the highest ethical feelings. But romantic love implies "neither the ethical relation of marriage or family."[22] All ethical relations can be justifiably sacrificed in the name of romantic love. It can cause men to perpetrate the most despicable and degrading acts.[23] In fact, the importance attributed to romantic love makes dissension and collision an inevitable part of human existence. This kind of love ignores or is indifferent to social laws and obligations. The interests of the state, church, and family conflict with the belief that it is all-powerful.[24]

Hegel asserts further that no other love is comparable to the kind that appears in the Christian era. The Greeks spoke of love, but referred either to the abstract, overly intellectual kind discussed by Plato or to the rational and respectable form exhibited by Penelope and Andromache. In the case of Paris and Helen the relationship is clearly a physical infatuation rather than a spiritual union. Similarly, Sappho's poetry is often filled with the language of love, but, as Hegel points out, love to her is also physical rather than spiritual.[25] The dramatists also never touch upon the love—whether divine or romantic—of Christianity. Neither Aeschylus nor Sophocles makes romantic love an important element in his plays. Antigone and Haemon, for example, may be lovers, but their love is never presented in any romantic way.[26] Haemon's suicide is never placed in the emotional and passionate light in which the romantic writers would have placed it. Where love does seem to have some significance, as in Euripedes' *Phaedra*, "it rather makes itself felt as a criminal aberration of the blood."[27]

None of these works is comparable to the Petrarchan son-
nets, for example, where, in spite of a certain amount of superficiality, there is a full development of all the emotional and
sensitive outpourings that accompany the feeling of love.
When art deals with divine love, as in much medieval painting
and in the great work of Dante, Petrarch, and even Boccaccio,
art attains its very highest success. But when the artist deals
with romantic love—love divorced from any religious significance—there is an essential shallowness in the work. For
this reason Shakespeare introduces religious overtones into
Romeo and Juliet in order to lend some universality to the
love story. For a similar reason, the great Greek plays, in spite
of their ineffective handling of romantic themes, will always
have universal appeal. The moral issues involved in conflicts
in romantic love can never have the same universal importance
as the moral issues in which Agamemnon, Clytemnestra, Orestes, Oedipus, Antigone, and Creon are implicated. The problems of love between two people are important and worth
serious consideration. But it is obvious that the struggles which
appear in the Greek plays are of much greater import. An unsuccessful love affair does not have the same profound implications as a violation of some implicit moral law. We are
fascinated more by Antigone than by Juliet.

> All men, it is true, should be sensitive to love and may claim satis-
> faction in this respect. But when a man fails to secure that object
> in some particular place, in precisely this or that association, under
> just these circumstances and in respect to one unique maiden we
> can admit no absolute wrong. There is nothing essentially inevi-
> table in the fact that a man should capriciously select any par-
> ticular young woman, and that we should interest ourselves con-
> sequently for that which is in the highest degree accidental, a
> caprice of his own conscious life, which carries with it no imper-
> sonal expansion or universal significance.[28]

Fidelity is the third important feature of medieval culture.
Originating out of the faith and trust expounded by the early
Christians, fidelity exemplifies a relationship that is no longer
the ideal of early Christianity. Fidelity cannot be equated with

friendship between equals, nor is it analogous to the love of a man for a woman. On the contrary, it implies a lack of equality in the relationship. Men who are equal in culture and intelligence bind themselves into a system of vassalage. Each vassal is usually a noble who, for reasons of his own, decides to give his services to another, more powerful noble. However, the bondage created always fluctuates between obedience and genuine freedom. Each vassal still retains his honor, his self-esteem, and the belief in the omnipotence of love. Thus, for example, in the *Cid* the hero is never strictly obligated to his king. If the king acts wrongly, if some personal offense is committed, then the Cid simply refuses to help. Similarly, in the *Reinecke Fuchs* the "superior lord commands, blusters, and scolds, but the independent and powerful individualities resist him precisely when and as they please."[29]

Fidelity, like honor and love, often leads to complete lack of trust. Each individual keeps faith only so long as his ego is not offended. For this reason Hegel rejects the view that looks back to the Middle Ages as the time of unity and synthesis:

> It really looks as though our chief praise of the Middle Ages must consist in this, that no man is in such a period justified in his own eyes or [is] a man of honour, except in so far as he runs after his own inclinations, in other words, does precisely that which he is not suffered to do in a State which is organized on a rational basis.[30]

These three values—honor, love, and fidelity—make up what is commonly known as the Chivalric Code. But, in Hegel's analysis, chivalry by no means exemplifies altruism and the spirit of good will. In fact, during the Middle Ages it deteriorates into a euphemism for actions that are essentially egotistical and arrogant. Moral action is no longer justified by reference to some objective criterion. All standards are capable of individual interpretation and, as a result, men make their own particular personalities the only source of justification. The assertion and accomplishment of individuality are their own vindication. Passion is made the basis of action without any reflection on the principles involved.[31] Individuals are now primarily regarded as autonomous and man's task is simply one of attempting to display this autonomy in all its facets.

This new social outlook is accompanied by an increase in artistic tempo. The artist finds himself drawn more and more into an interest in personality for its own sake. Even though Hegel deplores the loss of religious emphasis, he still recognizes and understands the tremendous appeal that the discovery of personality has for the artist. The great man may often be perverse, but in him can most easily be seen the explicit motion of the powers resident in human beings. This is what really fascinates us about the very strong personality. We see in him not an exemplar of truth and morality, but a symbol of an infinite number of mysterious forces which are buried in the being of man. Macbeth, Othello, and Richard III are not symbolic of great Christian truths. They are not moral beings. What makes them unique is the power they manifest. In them undreamt-of potentialities are realized. Macbeth, Hegel declares, is like the appearance of a sudden natural catastrophe whose meaning is incomprehensible but whose power is immediately felt. He exists as a kind of terrible god who is oblivious to everything else except his own creations.

> This regardless tenacity, this identity of the man [Macbeth] with himself, and the object which his own personality brings to birth is the source to him of an abiding interest. Nothing makes him budge, neither the respect for the sacredness of kingship, nor the madness of his wife, nor the rout of his vassals, nor destruction as it rushes upon him, neither divine nor human claims—he withdraws from them all into himself and persists.[32]

These characters of Shakespeare's are not comparable, according to Hegel, to the strong Greek heroes. First of all, the Greek hero is rarely as psychologically complex as Macbeth. Compared to Macbeth, Odysseus is perfectly understandable, even well-adjusted. Achilles, Philoctetes, and the other Greek heroes show their strength in their actions. We are never asked to enter into and to understand their thoughts and feelings. Secondly, the Greek hero is first and foremost an ethical being. Even though the ethical laws he signifies are never made explicit, there is little question that Achilles is essentially just, good, and heroic. We respect him because of the ideal picture of mankind that he represents. But we do not similarly respect the Shakespearean hero. He is devoid of the high moral virtues which could attract us. The power of his personality is itself sufficient to hold our interest.

Although not all of the heroes and heroines of the romantic age have the same dynamic quality as Macbeth, all of them are strongly concerned with self. Thus the Juliet of *Romeo and Juliet* reveals the same introspective character as Macbeth. Once she encounters Romeo, her passion is the only guiding element within her. Similarly, Shakespeare's Miranda and Schiller's Thekla have the same dynamic impetuosity. Though Thekla is placed "in the midst of a life of such amplitude and richness, she remains unaffected by it; she remains within it without vanity, without reflection, purely absorbed by the one interest which alone dominates her soul."[33] Hamlet, of course, is the exemplar of the introspective type. He "wanders astray without a strong grasp of life's realities. . . . He is not carried away with the flood, as Macbeth; he cannot either kill, rage, or strike with the directness of a Laertes; he persists in the inactivity of a beautiful, introspective soul."[34]

The advent of the self-absorbed hero who is motivated by passion and egotism rather than by any objective criteria not only introduces a new dramatic personality, but also causes a change in the conception of action. Aristotle believed that action was the most important element of the drama. Hence, the artist was required to have a good knowledge of the kind of actions allowable. The Greeks were very sensitive to the requirements of action. Its length and unity were very essential considerations. For Hegel, also, action is a vital component of drama. Even though the introspective hero represents an improvement over those whose personalities are never emphasized, he ought still to be represented in a determinate situation. The actualization of the potentialities of personality is still best expressed in action. For this reason even the romantic artist must deal with the problem of differentiating suitable from unsuitable actions. According to Hegel, Shakespeare is aware of this need to combine action with individuality. But as the Romantic Age progresses, the interest in the self-absorbed personality becomes so great that action becomes secondary. Any and all activities are indiscriminately used as appropriate vehicles for the introspective hero. The individual who has his honor to defend, for example, "is perfectly able to enter into any and every [situation] as it may chance to occur, to find himself the object of insult therein, or to look for an opportunity in which he may display his courage and shrewdness."[35] There no longer has to be a justifiable ground for action. "The judgment passed upon that which in every particular case is held to be right or wrong, is throughout relegated to the entirely haphazard criteria of individual judgment."[36]

The result of this indifferent attitude toward action is that fantasy and satire begin to characterize art. Since action and personality are no longer interdependent, the drama deteriorates rapidly. Once the medieval and especially the Renaissance artists make personality the touchstone for determining values rather than an objective set of standards, they begin to treat their art lightly. They no longer have the important task of giving concrete form to the great abstract forces that permeate man and nature. Both in Ariosto and Cervantes this influence begins to make its appearance. Although Ariosto can still depict courage, love, and honor, and all the noble passions, his heroes are frequently engaged "in what is often unadulterated folly and the wildest eccentricity."[37] He also often degrades the divine love of Dante or the romantic tenderness of Petrarch into "sensuous tales and ludicrous collisions."[38] Similarly in Cervantes' *Don Quixote* we have "a noble nature in whose adventures chivalry goes mad, the substance of such adventures being placed as the centre of a stable and well-defined state of things whose external character is copied with exactness from nature."[39] Don Quixote signifies what must finally occur when a man attempts to force his own personal views on all of mankind. By ignoring the need for universality in his views, he trips over actuality and thus becomes an object of ridicule.

Hegel admires both Ariosto and Cervantes, but he also feels that in their work, as well as in some of the plays of Shakespeare, especially in the scenes involving Falstaff, there appears the final dissolution of the romantic spirit. This dissolution is completed in Hegel's own age—the early part of the nineteenth century. His age has become so blasé and so unromantic that when artists "seek to make a Greek god or, as our own Protestants try to do, a Virgin Mary the object of a piece of sculpture or a picture, it is impossible for us to treat such a material with entire seriousness."[40] It might be argued that many modern novels contain the spirit of chivalry. But Hegel insists that such chivalry does not have the kind of individuality that truly exemplifies the romantic spirit. The hero of the modern novel shows individuality only in a social sense. He fights hard in order to make his place in society. But "the day comes at last with the most of us when the maiden is discovered and some kind of place in the world, he marries, and is as much a Philistine as the rest of his neighbours."[41] The true romantic spirit is dead.

The major question that now arises is this: If true romantic art is no longer satisfactory, then what is to replace it? Hegel contends that since art no longer has any specific, serious subject matter, it will revert to its earliest concern with everything. The downfall of chivalry, as well as the recognition that purely personal actions are not very meaningful, frees the artist from the search for specific situations. He is now able to represent everything, both of humanity and nature. Art "has become a free instrument which is qualified to exercise itself relatively to every content, no matter what kind it may be."[42] Art is no longer primarily concerned with the Idea. The implicit has become explicit. Hegel concludes that art can no longer develop further.

This remarkable conclusion has incited harsh criticism of Hegel's theory of art. Not only does Hegel seem to imply that art no longer has an intrinsic purpose, but also that it will finally be completely superseded by the more intellectual discipline of philosophy.[43] On one interpretation, the criticism made against Hegel is just. The development of inquiry into the nature of the Absolute reaches a point at which the Absolute can no longer be given an objective status. Since the Absolute now refers to what is intellectual, since there no longer is an external subject matter which is considered most adequate for representing the Idea, the artist's task would seem to be trivialized. Mind, with all of its potentialities for intellectual conceptualization, can best deal with the nature and explication of the Idea. Art, which exists only because it can give a concrete representation of an abstraction, is no longer satisfactory. Philosophy has reached the stage where it is aware that the most profound characteristics of mind and of the Absolute can be given only conceptually, not perceptually. Knowledge of God is a conceptual matter; no empirical content can adequately represent Him. This does not mean, however, that the Idea is an abstraction without concrete counterparts. Hegel always insisted that the validity of the Idea rests on its being definable in terms of concrete phenomena. However, the Idea itself, in its wholeness, can only be grasped by thought.

Perhaps we may best grasp Hegel's view by distinguishing between a plan of action and the means taken for its fulfillment. Although the plan may entail certain concrete consequences, we would undoubtedly distinguish between these consequences and the plan itself. The plan would be an intellectual conception which was being fulfilled in experience but which could not be adequately understood by simply observing the occurrence of one event after another. Real knowledge could come only when we understood the end or plan that was implicit in these events. Since the plan is to be distinguished from the given external events, and since art can only be concerned with external events, it followed for Hegel that art was, by its very nature, incapable of grasping the significance or Idea that permeates external phenomena. Art, therefore, must give way to those areas that can comprehend the Idea, namely, religion and, finally, philosophy. In such fashion Hegel justified his belief in the eventual depreciation of the intrinsic value of art.

However, Hegel's writings lend themselves to another interpretation, which does not place art in such an unfavorable position. Athough it is true that the artist can no longer represent the Absolute because the Absolute is now recognized to be essentially an intellectual concept, Hegel suggested that in the hands of a great mind art can still present unique insights into the nature of experience. Such an artist, who does not shun ideas, can call our attention to facets of experience which we might otherwise ignore. He can make us more conscious of higher values and more important problems. He can make objects more interesting to us by attaching to them "a deeper emotion, a sleight of witticism, an ingenious fancy, or a real flash of imaginative power."[44] Creations of this kind, Hegel asserted, are truly significant and worthy of attention. They add something to human experience that makes it more exhilarating and exciting to us.[45]

Thus, in the final analysis Hegel did not really reject art as an important element in human experience. Rather he seemed to be simply declaring that art can no longer convey to men those highest concepts that are given in religion and philosophy. Art may no longer be able to make the Idea concrete for us, but this does not mean that it cannot enrich human experience. The great artist, Hegel concluded, will always be able to lift "the soul high above all its painful perplexity into the ordered limits of the real."[46]

VI. THE ROMANTIC STAGE
OF ART: PAINTING

THE romantic arts are so important to Hegel, and his analysis
is so lengthy that the romantic cultural milieu and the specific
arts must be treated separately here. The following chapters
will be concerned with Hegel's comments on painting, music,
and poetry.

To understand the significance that Hegel attributes to
painting, reference must be made to the success and failure of
sculpture as an art. Sculpture is indeed much more successful
than architecture in the presentation of an aesthetic object
which can immediately arouse in men a feeling of the enigmatic and latent forces that reside in human beings. But the
very nature and material of sculpture limit its potentialities
for full expression. Sculpture cannot incorporate those subtle
qualities of the human personality that are to be found in the
living figure and the living face. The wise glance or the passionate expression cannot be adequately presented by sculpture.[1] Nor is it able to "represent actions involving motion,
and which imply collision of opposing forces."[2] All the psychological and intellectual struggles that man undergoes in his
desire to make explicit within him all that is implicit cannot
be incorporated by the medium of sculpture. In the Niobe and
Laocoön groups there is a sense of despair and lamentation,
but the very medium itself restricts the full expression of the

suffering that is being endured.[3] It remains for painting to give a fuller representation of the Idea as it makes its appearance in experience. It is painting, as the first art in the Romantic Age, which captures the life that permeates man and which endeavors to pictorialize it.[4] The potentialities merely implicit in the first forms of life are now depicted in vivid actuality. In observing a painting, Hegel declares, "we are at once and for the first time conscious in it of the principle of our finite and yet essentially infinite spiritual substance, the life and breath of our own existence; we contemplate in its pictures the very spark which works and is active in ourselves."[5] Unlike architecture or sculpture, painting can exhibit to us some of man's most intimate thoughts. It "makes the *soul* of man itself the subject of its creative work."[6]

However, it is not the task of the painter to deal with all emotions. He looks for those which seem to suggest something godly in man and then he endeavors to externalize these emotions in a permanent form. For this reason the painter can never be called an imitator. Plato was wrong. The painter captures in his imagination that one fleeting moment in which suddenly men are not simply social, political, or economic animals, but beings endowed with certain strange and marvellous powers. This is a difficult job. The moment is elusive and memory is often weak. But the great artist can nurture this moment and finally set it down so that all can feel its impact.

Unlike sculpture, painting does not reach its peak in the cultural milieu of ancient Greece. Although there is evidence that painting was also a part of Greek art, Hegel denied that such paintings could possibly have been comparable to the art of the Middle Ages, and pre-eminently the art of the sixteenth and seventeenth centuries. The Greeks could not grasp the intimacy and depth of emotion that are present in Christianity. The Greek artist did not see in emotion anything more than a sign of a strange madness or illness in man. Of course the Greeks did appreciate the pleasures of mind and body. But their stress on balance and self-restraint made strong emotional expression a thing to be shunned.

There is a Greek painting of young Bacchus, carried by a faun and tended by nymphs, which depicts a sentiment of unrestrained love for a child. But compare this scene with that in Christian paintings where love of the Christ Child is represented. The Greek expression "possesses in no respect the intimacy, the depth of soul, which confront us in Christian paintings."[7] Sculpture was much more suitable than painting for expressing the rationalistic and restrained outlook of Greek civilization.[8]

The lack of emotional depth is not only apparent in the fragments of Greek painting, but even more so in Egyptian painting. The ancients, Hegel conceded, may have painted excellent portraits, "but neither their way of conceiving natural fact, nor the point of view from which they regarded human and divine conditions was of the kind that, in the case of painting, an infusion of soul-life could be expressed with such intimate intensity as was possible in Christian painting."[9] We have only to examine one Egyptian painting found in bas-relief which portrays Isis with Horus on her knees. The subject matter is identical with the Madonna pictures that were painted by Raphael and other Italian masters, but the Egyptian Isis "has nothing maternal about her, no tenderness, no trait of soul or emotion, such as is not even wholly absent in the stiffer Byzantine pictures of the Madonna."[10] There is no comparison between the depth and profundity of emotion presented by the Egyptian work and that presented by the work of Raphael.

Byzantine art is an improvement over its predecessors in that at least it is aware of the need to place some emphasis on the psychological and introspective features of men. But it also, according to Hegel, is not very satisfactory. Byzantine painting, with its Greek tradition, exemplifies the stiffness and lifelessness of Greek painting. "The modelling, by means of light and shadow, brilliance and obscurity, and their fusion, no less than perspective and the art of lifelike grouping, either were not elaborated at all, or to a very small extent."[11] Furthermore, suffering is portrayed more in a physical than in a psychological sense.

The Byzantine influence began to wane with the advance of Italian art. Thus, even though early painters, such as Duccio, the artists of Siena, and Cimabue of Florence, still used many Greek elements, they brought more warmth and spiritual quality into their figures.[12] Finally, in Giotto, an apprentice of Cimabue, the dominance of the Byzantine style was minimized. Human emotions and concrete representation became important to him. He introduced "the truth and grace of nature . . . [and] concentrated his attention on what is present and actual, and compared the forms and effects which he undertook to exhibit with Life as it existed around him."[13] However, Hegel tempered his praise with the assertion that Giotto, in spite of the impetus he gave to art, must not be considered one of the truly great. In the tendency of Giotto to humanize and to produce realism "he never really, as a rule, advances beyond a comparatively subordinate stage in the process."[14]

The development of individuality and interest in the human personality continues into the fifteenth century with Masaccio and Fra Angelico. But it is with the rise of such great masters as Da Vinci, Raphael, Correggio, and Titian that painting reaches its highest peak. Although Masaccio had already solved the problem of chiaroscuro, Da Vinci and Correggio perfected it. Giotto tried to fuse emotion with the formalism of the Greeks. But Da Vinci and Raphael finally create the perfect fusion.

> By virtue of his artistic thoroughness, his almost over-refined passion for detail, his exquisite delicacy of mind and feeling. [Da Vinci] not only penetrated further than any other into the mysteries of the human form and the secrets of its expression but, through his equally profound knowledge of all the techniques of a painter, attained to an extraordinary infallibility in the employment of all the means that his researches and practice had placed within his reach.[15]

Raphael received similar praise. In him we find united "the highest ecclesiastical feeling for the themes of religious art and a complete knowledge and enthusiastic respect for natural phenomena in all the animation of their color and shape together with an insight fully as great for the beauty of the antique."[16] Correggio and Titian are also praised even though they do not attain the greatness of Da Vinci and Raphael.

By referring to numerous painters and schools of painting, Hegel attempted to corroborate his significant generalization that romantic—especially medieval and Renaissance—painting could never be surpassed. New arts may develop which will undoubtedly be more meaningful to men. But Hegel argued that in terms of the particular genre, romantic painting represents the highest development the art can undergo.

When we turn now to an analysis of some of the specific characteristics of romantic painting we find that the emphasis is on subject matter. The medieval artist, for example, never for a moment doubts that religious concepts ought to form the intellectual content of his work. As we have seen, the life of Christ, the various events relating to His death and resurrection, serve to give the painter concrete images which he could feel certain actually displayed the Idea. The picture of God, the Madonna, and especially the figure of Christ, both at birth and death, are frequently found in medieval painting. But even though the medieval painter had a storehouse of religious material from which to pick, his task was an easy one. The knowledge and maturity required to represent an image of God was considerable. How was God to be presented to the religious imagination of Christendom? The Greeks had their Zeus, but for Christianity, God as spiritual personality and Supreme Power was "only retained as such without defined form and as an abstraction of thought."[17] The same sense of contradiction that permeated the Greek attempt to fuse infinitude and finitude also appeared in the medieval attempts to represent God. "However broad in its generalization, however lofty, ideal, and masterful the presentment of such a figure may be, we fail to get beyond the fact that it is entirely a human individual of more or less grave aspect, which fails entirely to coalesce with the conception of God the Father."[18] Even the great Van Eycks, whom Hegel very much admired, could not create an adequate portrait of God. In their best attempt—probably the altar picture at Ghent—"our imagination cannot fail to find something in it which does not satisfy."[19]

Hence the Christ figure becomes a more suitable subject for painting. But, as we have seen previously, it is no easy matter to do justice to the figure and personality of Christ. Christ can not be described simply as a wise man, one who is, therefore, to be painted with the facial expression that characterizes the wise men appearing in Raphael's "School of Athens." Christ was indeed wise, but He was also much more. Nor is Christ adequately presented to us by the heads painted by Van Eyck and Memling, because in these works He is made to appear too human. The meaning of Christ is such that a satisfactory portrayal would have to take into account the fact that He is both man and God. The artist's problem becomes one of producing a figure which is at once human and Godlike. Nor could the expression of the face be merely a human expression of compassion and pity. Again, this would make Christ appear as merely an exceptionally wise human being. It is the artist's task to paint a Christ figure with both ideal and human qualities. For this reason Van Eyck's paintings of the Christ Child are not adequate. They "are in general stiff and emphasize the defective form of the newly-born child."[20] However, the examples of the Christ Child which appear in Raphael's pictures, especially the Child that appears in the Sistine Madonna painting at Dresden, are more successful. They "offer us the most beautiful presentment of childhood."[21]

The artist, therefore, must have an awareness of the beliefs of Christianity if he is to gain any insight into the religious feelings he seeks to express. But in addition he must be sensitive to those distinctions which make one personality seem to be more profound and more religious than another. He must have the talent of presenting the concrete expressions that best signify religious emotions. In real life, Hegel pointed out, we frequently have difficulty in recognizing whether a particular contortion of the human face signifies fear or happiness. Similarly, the face of an old man is sometimes strangely twisted "because the lines of [his] features are too pronounced, cold, and stiff to accommodate themselves readily to an unreserved and natural laugh or to a friendly smile."[22] A facial movement is not always allied to an emotion. But painting should as far as possible seek to "produce a harmony between the soul and its external mode of expression."[23] The Italians were able to achieve this harmony to a much higher degree than either the German or the Flemish painters.

Allied to the artistic concern with Christ and His personal life are other religious subjects which interest the artist. Prayer, for example, is an important element in many medieval paintings. But Hegel warned that painting a person at prayer is not an easy matter. A keenly observant artist will be able to see the difference between the expressions of one who sincerely indulges in prayer and one who does so hypocritically. Some artists have utilized certain set expressions in order to convey the impression of prayerfulness or saintliness, such as the lifting of the eyes heavenward. But this technique may not be appropriate under certain conditions. When the lifting of the eyes is no longer a spontaneous trait suggesting saintliness, but is used artificially, it "is somewhat too near to our modern sentimentalism."[24] The artist must constantly be sensitive to expressions that are no longer fresh and original.

Again some painters have believed that the effect of great spiritual quality is attained by showing some form of human sacrifice or courage under great duress. For this reason paintings of martyrs were very common among medieval artists. But if an artist is not careful, such a subject matter can destroy the spiritual effect that is desired. Emphasis on physical pain makes us oblivious to the spiritual message. "The endurance of martyrs in physical tortures is an endurance which carries with it merely physical pain: what the spiritual Ideal looks for is the trial of the soul in its own domain, its own peculiar suffering, the wounds of its love, the repentance, mourning, anguish, and penance of its heart."[25] The most important artists of the medieval period spent much time obtaining a perfect sketch of the human body. But these sketches only served as an instrument to communicate a further meaning. They were never an end in themselves. On the other hand, paintings that emphasize torture and the like can easily be subverted to a mere interest in the physical for its own sake.

Although religious themes are most interesting for romantic artists, they make some attempts to employ other subjects. Hence we note that Raphael, Rubens, and Correggio sometimes use mythological topics in their painting, but such work is successful only because the artist succeeds in infusing a Christian view into the content. Hegel was convinced that an artist could not divorce himself from his cultural milieu. He could not deal with values and conceptions that he no longer felt. He might try to go back into the past and absorb the attitudes and beliefs of that era. But always, either consciously or unconsciously, he would view the past in terms of the present. For this reason the artist would do better to involve himself in his own rather than in another culture. One can never "recall to life . . . past history."[26]

Again, some painters during the medieval period looked to nature for inspiration rather than to purely religious contexts. But it is never nature per se that enlists the artist's interest, but nature as he invests it with his own moods and emotions. In the paintings of nature there is to be found "the *vitality* and soul imported into them by the artist's conception and execution, his emotional life in fact, which is reflected in his work, and gives us not merely a counterfeit of external objects, but therewith his own personality and temperament."[27] In short, when the artist seems to be imitating nature he is really *using* nature in order to express some fundamental feeling. Natural phenomena are changed, under artistic inspiration, from purely external objects into instruments for creating a religious mood in an observer.

A number of artists also dealt with the commonplace and with everyday existence, but for them the commonplace is never a mere imitation of reality. The artist does not paint *any* scene or *any* event. He selects the scenes and events that he wishes to re-create, and his criteria for selection are ideal. What he wishes to do is to capture those rare moments when men act and react in accordance with some principle that he considers ideal. For this reason artists of this kind could be concerned with practically any subject matter, since ideal activity can make its appearance anywhere. But for the same reason the content of such paintings always runs the risk of being misunderstood or of being appreciated for other than aesthetic reasons.

Paintings about some practical or everyday occurrence very often make us react in a practical fashion. If the subject matter touches upon some important need, then we like it. If it does not, then we do not like it. But this kind of practical attitude toward art destroys the possibility of an aesthetic experience. Art then becomes no more than a means to something else that is really important. There is no appreciation for the art work per se. The practical attitude prevails in most of our dealings with others and with the external world at large. But the intention of art is to erase this practical attitude.

Whereas we rarely see an entire event because we are so much concerned with that aspect of the event which has practical consequences for us, art seeks to develop and nourish an attitude that will permit us to take a detached view of an event. Painting, Hegel declared, may present us with a scene that is similar to what we experience every day, but "it furthermore destroys all the threads of practical necessity, attraction, inclination, or disinclination, which draw us to such a Present, or the reverse, and forces us to approach those objects more intimately as ends to themselves in their own particular phase or mode of life."[28]

Painting, therefore, can attach permanence to *momentary* things. The sudden moment of poignancy, of great sacrifice, can be made eternal by the power of the painting.[29]

> Concrete reality is so overburdened with the phenomenal, that is incidental or accidental detail, that we frequently cannot see the forest for the trees, and often the most important fact slips by us as a thing of common or daily occurrence. It is the indwelling insight and genius of the [artist] which first adds the quality of greatness to events or actions, presenting them fully in a truly historical composition, which rejects what is purely external, and only brings into prominence that through which that ideal substance is vitally unfolded.[30]

Finally, the medieval and Renaissance artists often engaged simply in portrait painting. Although portraits cannot, according to Hegel, be as fascinating as religious scenes, still they can attain great artistic beauty. A talented painter can give us a glimpse into the inner personality of a man. By a slight change in an eyebrow or in some other facial characteristic, he can catch and immortalize a man's real personality. The painter "makes visible the unique impression of any personality by seizing and emphasizing precisely those traits . . . and parts in which this distinctive personal quality is expressed in its clearest and most vitally pregnant embodiment."[31] For this reason a portrait may be very true to nature, sketched with precision and perseverance, and yet not be as good as another portrait, which may be a mere sketch but "infinitely more vivacious and arresting in its truth."[32] Titian's portraits are probably the best portrait paintings. The impression we get from his work "is that of a complete personality. We get from them an idea of spiritual vitality, such as actual experience is unable to supply."[33] Dürer can also present in his art an individual's real inner personality, "his most unique and intimate self."[34] But too often portrait painting is no more than an imitation of the superficial personality man wears as a mask in his society. The amiable little smile that is often found in a portrait is no doubt pleasant "but the merely polite amiability of social intercourse is not a fundamental trait of any character, and becomes in the hands of many artists only too readily the most insipid kind of sweetness."[35]

As in sculpture so in painting, the techniques used are also very important. An incorrect drawing of a line or a curve can suddenly create an undesirable impression. A deficient knowledge of the laws of perspective or of balance can trivialize the most significant concept. But the most important technique involves the use of color. In the final analysis, Hegel declared, an artist can make magnificent sketches with masterful balance and symmetry. But if he is unable to use color and to be sensitive to its various nuances, it is highly improbable that he can become a great painter.

Thus, for example, while the drawings of Raphael and Dürer are excellent—in fact, the border drawings of Dürer in the Prayer Book of the Munich Library are of "indescribable ideality and freedom"[36]—such work cannot really be compared to that which makes great use of color. It is only through "its employment of colour that the art of painting is able to give a real and vital presentment to the wealth of soul-life."[37] Except for Correggio and a few other Italian artists, the Dutch and Flemish painters were the superior colorists.[38]

As Hegel pointed out, colors are truly remarkable phenomena. Like words, they are capable of being given an indefinite number of meanings and of arousing a variety of emotions. Like words, also, they can be used in order to produce a fresh meaning or a new emotional reaction. The gifted artist is as sensitive to colors as the gifted writer is sensitive to words. Similarly, both seek to use language or hues in such a way that an original idea, meaning, or insight is suddenly revealed. When the painter uses colors he does not simply see dabs of soft material that are to be placed on canvas. Just as the writer must master the meanings that phrases can have, so also the painter must master the meanings that colors can have. Thus when the old masters wanted to convey moods of tranquillity and contemplation, they used blue because this color was most apt to be associated with the mood which prevails when we observe the blueness of the heavens.[39] Red, with its brightness and its associative tie to the swift flow of blood, was used to signify masculinity, glory, and dominance. When the medieval artists wished to stress the maternal element in the Virgin Mary they garbed her in a blue cloak, but when they wanted to emphasize the fact that she was the Queen of Heaven her clothing was red.

Along with the sensitivity to colors there is a concomitant sensitivity to color harmony. Hegel was convinced that the truly great painting signified an ordered system of colors. Some color combinations were unsatisfactory. They were not "articulated system[s]."[40] Hegel maintained that a logical system was not complete if it did not include a specific set of axioms. Similarly, if a painting did not include the four cardinal hues, blue, yellow, red, and green, it could not be very successful.[41] Furthermore, Hegel believed that there were specific rules of contrast and balance that had to be followed. Some color schemes led to too sharp a contrast or emphasis; others were too innocuous. There were no rules for the creation of a masterpiece, but Hegel thought that there were some techniques the artist was required to use.

Hegel was aware that creating different shades of color was a major problem. The artist usually wished to enchant his audience by giving a new tone to an old color. But obtaining a different and yet effective shade of red or blue was a remarkably difficult problem. A good example of such a problem, Hegel asserted, can be seen in the artistic attempt to obtain the color of flesh, which, as painted, seems to be a curious combination of all colors without any single hue being prominent. But few artists have been able to create a color which would signify real living flesh, and, Hegel observes, the artist who finally achieves this will achieve great fame.

The painter, therefore, must have an awareness both of the rules and regulations of his trade as well as of the concepts and ideas of his culture, although Hegel admits that the conceptual and ideational framework of the painting is the most important. An artist who is not sensitive to and who does not appreciate knowledge and intellectual accomplishments cannot be very good. In fact, satisfactory conceptual subject matter can often serve to compensate for deficient technique. Thus, Raphael's cartoons are highly regarded because of their subject matter, not because of their technique, which is excelled in most respects by that of the Dutch masters.[42] No matter how excellent technique may be, it can never bring greatness to a painting if the concepts are not significant or well understood. Hence Hegel would probably have rejected much of contemporary abstract art, or perhaps have pointed to it as the logical result of an art that no longer has any intellectual subject matter. Even though he sometimes speaks appreciatively of harmony and symmetry, like Kant he makes such beauty subordinate to the far more important beauty which at least appears to deal with recognizable concepts.[43]

As the Romantic Age wanes, art begins to interest itself in secular rather than religious matters. The Dutch and German schools begin to deal exclusively with the ordinary man as he lives his ordinary life. This change signifies the deterioration of painting as the art form which best expresses men's most profound beliefs. The artist now becomes indifferent to the concepts of his day. Since God is not easily expressible in the painting, since man's feelings and psychological motivations cannot be adequately presented in terms of imagery, the painter turns from profound ideas to ordinary scenes. But now he no longer feels the drive toward attaining the highest perfection. He is no longer dealing with a subject matter that inherently forces him to exert the greatest care and dexterity. For this reason even technique begins to suffer, so that finally the age gives us not only ordinary art, but also bad technique. Hegel depreciated the artistic endeavors of his own age:

> Our artist only too frequently will confront us with portraits and historical pictures, at which we have only to cast a bare glance, and we see that, while flatly contradicting the wildest dream of

what is possible in mankind or anyone in particular, he neither knows aught at all about mankind or his natural color, nor yet the modes of composition in which we may justly express that humanity.[44]

Painting has now run its course. Only a medium which can give greater insight into the human personality and the divinity that resides there can revitalize art and renew its importance.

VII. THE ROMANTIC STAGE
OF ART: MUSIC

In the last chapter we saw that Hegel believed painting to be a more successful art form than either architecture or sculpture in depicting those inner emotions and feelings which suggest the play of the Idea in man.[1] However, in spite of its great capacity, painting "is unable to give us the development of a situation, event, or action, as poetry or music, that is to say, in a *series* of changes."[2] It can present us with a moment of an event, but not with an event in its entirety. Furthermore, painting can image for us only the more obvious emotions. It deals only with emotions that have a *"definite* mode of expression."[3] But painting cannot be concerned with those subtle emotions which are not expressed in any physical part of the human body. Frustration, loneliness, and even love, cannot be defined by strict reference to some set of physiological characteristics. For this reason the painter's medium is necessarily deficient. It cannot present to us some of men's most vital feelings. For the painter every psychological mood must have a physical counterpart. But, according to Hegel, there are some psychological moods which are never given outward expression. Painting is inherently incapable of ever touching upon an entire area of important psychological phenomena.

In music, Hegel declared, many of these deficiencies are overcome. First of all, music is able to arouse the most subtle and varied emotions. It can stimulate us more than painting and create a much more profound religious feeling. Secondly, music can give us the emotional reaction that often accompanies ideal events. During such events emotions go through stages of development from beginning to completion. The determinate action, for example, incorporates a developing emotion that makes us look forward to the completion of the action at the conclusion. Painting cannot give us this kind of emotional reaction. But music is permeated by the patterns of beginning, middle, and end. When we listen to music our feelings go through a stage of development so that we are frustrated when the composition ends at an inappropriate time.

This emotional response touches upon the most significant aspect of the human personality. Great music does not stir up images or memories even though this may occur incidentally. What it does is to stimulate the pattern of dialectic that every human consciousness possesses. Unlike painting, Hegel argued, music ignores imagery, that is, the contents of the categories of consciousness. It makes a direct appeal to the categories themselves. Kant was right when he thought of art as a stimulant to the forms of the mind.[4] But the forms of the mind, according to Hegel, must be thought of in the evolutionary fashion—thesis, antithesis, and synthesis. For this reason, when we hear music that corresponds to this pattern, we have an immediate reaction. We are moved psychologically in the same way that various rhythmic patterns are able to affect material objects.

Thirdly, music, unlike painting, is almost completely devoid of any but an aesthetic appeal. Since music does not rely upon imagery there is little danger that we can confuse a pragmatic with an aesthetic interest. Music "forsakes the element of external form and its sensuous *visibility*."[5] Painting, by its very presentation of physical objects and scenes, can easily distract attention from what is ideal and vital. On the other hand, music does not contain such distraction. By being divorced from imagery music forces us to turn into our inner selves. It does this by appealing to the ear rather than to the eye. The eye, Hegel argues, gives us impressions which can have an immediate pragmatic use. We can mistake the intrinsic value of the actual field of wheat for the intrinsic value of the painted field of wheat. But the impressions of the ear have no such immediate connection to possible use. Thus when we appreciate music we cannot really be mistaken in our motives. We can still be trapped into saying we enjoy music which we do not really enjoy, just as we can with any art. But when we genuinely enjoy music we cannot be confusing such enjoyment with the pleasure that occurs when we regard an object which can be useful to us. The pragmatic cannot play as important a role in music as it does in painting.

The artistic advantage of music over the other arts is also clearly observed when we compare it to sculpture and architecture. Its advantage over sculpture is quite obvious. "A figure, for example, in a plastic work of art, requires in this or that situation a body, hands, feet, bust, a head with a given expression, a given pose, other figures, or other aspects to which it is related as a whole, etc., and all these aspects presuppose the others, in making collectively essentially complete work."[6] But, as we have seen, the musical work does not obtain its unity by a reliance on external objects. The significance of music rests on its highly abstract organization. Without imagery it directly stimulates the evolving force in our own being. Not only is the important sense of action missing in sculpture, but also our attention is constantly being directed toward some non-aesthetic object. The work reminds us of someone, or else we are attracted simply to the bronze or the marble. On the other hand, music has removed many of these limitations. Even though we can no longer deal with images, we do obtain the full sense of evolving action with its emotional accompaniment. In essence, music stimulates the form or process that is implicit in all human experience without committing us to any specific set of images.

It is important to recognize that music, painting, and the other arts have many similarities. All these arts have various rules of symmetry and harmony that must be followed. According to Hegel, there are specific combinations of colors, tones, and so on, which immediately will be regarded with disapproval. Just as certain chemicals destroy flesh, so also certain sets of sounds or colors will automatically make an unpleasant impression on the mind. Furthermore, especially in music and architecture, there is a definite commitment to the use of mathematical laws.[7] Sounds could be defined in terms of mathematical relations from which we could infer the consistency or inconsistency of a particular arrangement of tones. Following such laws, however, is a necessary but not a sufficient condition for the creation of great music. The true musician requires more than a good knowledge of mathematics if he is to produce the best type of music. He must know which out of all possible arrangements of sounds can stimulate the most profound emotions.

Hegel endeavors to elaborate on his conception of the relation of emotions to music. He points out that we ought not to think that it is the purpose of music to arouse hates or fears or various physical desires. Such stimulation is incidental to the major aim of music. Following Kant, Hegel argues that some human feelings are not specifically related to any physical or pragmatic need. The disinterested interest that Kant mentioned is a good example of this curious feeling that men sometimes undergo. Such feelings are derived from something much more fundamental than a mere physical desire. They seem, instead, to be due to an element in us that is free of material want and which grows out of the needs of the abstract being that permeates us. This force, this soul in us, requires just as much of a fulfillment as the physical body in which this force resides. In Hegel's words, music touches "our entirely empty ego, the self without further content."[8] Food can satiate the body. Various visual impressions can be soothing to the eye. But music satiates the abstract life-force that is in the body and that acts as a receiver of all sense impressions. For this reason the aesthetic, as well as the religious, emotion is for Hegel a unique and unforgettable experience. It literally involves the most essential aspect of our being.

> The unique function of music consists in this, that whatever its content may be it is not so created by the art for human apprehension as though it either was held by consciousness as a *general concept* is so contained, or as definite external form is ordinarily presented to our perception, or as such receives its more complete reflection in the artistic counterfeit, but rather in the way in which a content is made a living thing in the sphere of the *personal soul.*[9]

In essence, music calls our attention to the importance of the Ego, of personality, in giving form and meaning to all possible experiences. In fact, it is the human tone itself, rather than facial expressions or any external features which most intimately and most clearly conveys to us man's inner being. The cry of grief, the sigh, the laugh are the most effective means for revealing the inner crises and personality of man. Tone is an immediate internal expression of feeling which requires no other external agent for interpretation.

Music is probably most similar to poetry. Both employ rhythm and harmony to attain their effects. But whereas in music ideas are subservient to rhythm, harmony, and emotion, in poetry the exact converse is true. Furthermore, in music the emotional appeal is divorced from specific ideas and images. In poetry, emotional appeal is usually embedded in specific ideas and images. For this reason poetry is a higher art than music. Poetry not only presents us with the universal emotions that sometimes appear in men but also with the concrete developing situations in which such emotions become expressed. In a sense it can be said that music gives us the pure feeling that can be experienced when we are engaged in great and significant activities. But it is poetry that can combine both feeling and activity. Music gives us the abstract universal; poetry gives us the concrete universal. In poetry "our emotions pass more completely out of their elementary medium of undefined conscious life into the more concrete vision and more universal imagination which is embodied in such content."[10] A musical composition may also do this when it is aided by language. But it is not the music per se that can indicate for us a specific genuine action. Some other art is required. No specific ideas or meanings can be disclosed "by virtue of the artistic elaboration of musical tones."[11]

Therefore, even though music cannot show us genuine actions, it ought always to deal with the emotions that attach to such actions. But Hegel admitted that there is some sense in speaking of music for its own sake. Some musical compositions are good exercises in rhythm, harmony, or even the physical ability to express various tone combinations. Such work is interesting in that it can be instrumental in training the artist for the production of a really important musical work. But we ought not to consider these musical exercises as significant in themselves, for their aim is not to stimulate any profound emotions. Thus in such works "music is empty, without significance, and is, for the reason that one fundamental aspect of art, namely spiritual content and expression, is absent, not really genuine music at all."[12] When music is deliberately divorced from any endeavor to communicate an important facet of man's experience, then it becomes a trivial pursuit. The enjoyment that such art affords is primarily pragmatic in that we admire the techniques employed rather than any fundamental significance in the work as a whole. Our interest is "only an interest in the purely musical characteristics of the composition and its artistic dexterity, an aspect which wholly concerns the musical expert, and is less connected with the universal human interest in art."[13]

In the opera a deliberate attempt is made to fuse music and poetry. But when such combinations occur, caution is necessary. The emotion expressed by the music may not always be compatible with the emotion expressed in the poetry. The fact that music is devoid of specific imagery does not signify that it is utilizable with any set of images that may be supplied. Furthermore, if both the poetry and the music contain strong emotional qualities the work as a whole may suffer. The audience will be torn between hearing the music and listening to the poetry. For these reasons Schiller's poems, because of their excellence, "have been shown to be ill adapted and indeed useless for musical composition."[14] On the other hand, the libretto for Mozart's *Magic Flute,* a collaboration by Emmanuel Schikaneder and Johann Georg Metzler (Gieseche), is, in spite of various deficiencies, one of "the best of opera librettos."[15] Its mystic references, its mysteries, are rather artificial, but "when combined with the depth, the bewitching loveliness and soul of the music it expands and floods our imagination, and warms the heart."[16]

The use of Old Latin texts with religious music has also produced highly successful syntheses. Similarly, the libretti of the operas of Gluck were perfectly adapted for music. The emotional quality of the music and the action described in the libretto were perfectly suited to one another. However, the emotional character of the libretti of Rossini is frequently entirely incompatible with the emotion expressed in the music.

> Only too often Rossini says goodbye to his libretto, and gives free vent to his melodies, precisely as his mood dictates; so that we have nothing left but to stick to the subject matter and grumble over the music that is indifferent to it, or abandon the former and take our hearty delight in the inspired irrelevances of the composer and the soul which they reveal.[17]

There is another important characteristic of music that must not be overlooked: that it takes place in time, not in space. Painting, like sculpture, can be observed spatially. A spectator "may observe this or that aspect of it; he may analyze the whole . . . , may make it the object of various reflections, and in short remain throughout at liberty to continue his independent review of it."[18] But the musical work takes place strictly in time. The unity that is felt requires a much greater mental effort than the unity observed in painting or sculpture. The listener must remember the sounds that have passed and then combine them with the sounds that are occurring. When a spectator examines a painting he can hold the immediate stimulus constantly before him. But in music it is impossible to refresh one's memory by referring back to sounds that have passed. They cannot be recalled again as active and immediate sense perceptions; they must be held in memory and related to present and future tones. Thus music, Hegel maintains, is the first art that gives us the sense of unification occurring in time rather than in space. It introduces us to a unity which permeates human consciousness, but which is only partly recognized in it. In Hegel's analysis the most significant unity is not that of substance underlying its attributes, but of process underlying its phases. An investigation of the things in experience is not as important as an investigation of its evolution and the moments of completion that frequently occur. We ought to know more about what is meant when we refer to the beginnings, the middles, and the ends in experience.

Music calls attention to the existence and future possibilities of such unities. It appeals to what was termed by Kant the inner sense, time, rather than the outer sense, space, and for this reason is a more profound art than painting. But this does not entail that every musical work is, therefore, inherently superior. The fact that unities are permeated by time does not mean that time is permeated by unities. Some music gives us the sense of pattern, but not necessarily the feeling of fulfillment or completion. Only the truly able musician can find the key that arouses this feeling. While various rules of harmony are usually followed by the musician, none of these rules can guarantee the production of a fine musical composition. As in all the arts, the musical genius supplies the crucial unknown element that results in the highest kind of music.

If we were asked specifically what it is that arouses us in music, we should undoubtedly answer that it is the beat or rhythm. Even the worst kind of music, if it has any rhythmical pattern, will make us react in some way. This reaction, Hegel says, is due to the conception of time that permeates experience. Just as music is made up of patterns of individual tones which rise and fall in accordance with a consistent beat, so time is definable in terms of a consistent flow of Nows, among which some attain more significance than others. Usually we are unaware of the mere flow of time, in the same way that we are unaware of our heartbeat. A drug, however, or even close attention, is able to make us conscious of it, and similarly music can make us aware of the rhythmic pattern that characterizes consciousness. Thus we actually become aware of an element essential to human psychology.

> Inasmuch, then, as Time and not the spatial condition as such supplies the essential element, in which tone secures existence in respect to its validity as music, and the time of tone is likewise that of the conscious subject, for this reason, tone, by virtue of its fundamental condition, penetrates into the self of conscious life, seizes hold of the same in virtue of the most simple aspect of its existence, and places the Ego in movement by means of the motion in Time and its rhythm.[19]

However, this fact—that time can be characterized as an infinite series of Nows following one another eternally and inevitably—is not sufficient to account for our discrimination between ordinary and extraordinary music. The steady beat, by its alliance to the beat implicit in human consciousness, does make us react and take notice. But such recurrence of sound does not account for the much more complex reaction that is effected when we listen to what we consider to be the most profound kind of music. Time has significant Nows, and music, if it is to be more than simply an appeal to the rhythmic pattern that permeates mind, must be able to suggest this qualitative distinction among Nows.

In order to produce this distinction, variations are added to the basic beat; stress and accent, for instance, are given to the individual tones. In this way, music begins to imitate human experience, in which time is usually accompanied by the rise and fall of emotional surges. The variations in tones and beats stimulate in us feelings similar to those that accompany significant and profound moments in our lives.[20] The laws of dissonance and consonance are derived from the fact that experience itself develops and deteriorates, undergoes periods of the utmost satisfaction or dissatisfaction. Therefore, by means of the dissonant seventh and ninth chords, music is able to "express the ideal significance no less than the purely subjective emotion of the profoundest content, that of religion, for example, and above all that of the Christian religion, in which the profoundest depth of suffering is an essential constituent."[21] Such dissonance gives us a sense of contradiction that demands resolution in the same way that religion often presents us with a contradiction which demands resolution.[22] The time beat, or organized combination of beats, stimulates recognition in consciousness of the unity that is sought amidst diversity.[23]

Hegel recognized that the laws of dissonance and consonance do not have the same kind of objectivity that the laws of the various sciences do. In architecture the most fundamental laws are sometimes legitimately violated in accordance with some "mysterious eurhythmy."[24] Similarly, the mathematical rules followed by musical compositions are sometimes deliberately violated. Music frequently "strides into and emphasizes the profound opposition that exists between this free life of soul and those quantitative relations on which it is based."[25]

The possibility of such deliberate violations ought not to surprise us. In the case of scientific laws we are dealing with nature, and in this connection man is unable to make a deliberate effort to change such laws. But in the case of the laws that are said to hold for art products one of the variables is consciousness. We are seeking to formulate a relationship not between two objective phenomena but between a phenomenon and a human consciousness. Thus laws of art are dependent upon changes in consciousness. As mind evolves, the kind of enjoyment we can have undergoes change. Laws become modified and even rejected. As the implicit dialectic of consciousness is made explicit, as mind becomes aware of its own tendency to affirm and negate and synthesize, more and more demands are made upon the kind of music that is being offered. A mind that has attained intellectual insight cannot be satisfied by the music which satisfies the unenlightened mind.

The rules of art, therefore, can never be so strict that the variable of consciousness can be ignored. However, some generalizations can be made. For example, no pattern of sounds ought to be continually reiterated. In many popular melodies, Hegel pointed out, one finds only a monotonous rhythm that is meant to represent the sentimental feelings occurring in unsuccessful love affairs.[26] At the same time there ought to be at least one strictly controlled pattern of sounds that is dominant throughout the composition. What is required in music is "a freedom from the pedantry of metre and the barbarism of a uniform rhythm."[27] But this prime requirement does not imply freedom from all restraints. "Music is Spirit or soul, which ring forth in their untrammelled immediacy, and derive satisfaction in this record of their self-knowledge. As a fine art, however, it is its necessary function to regulate the expression of such life no less than its effects"[28] In the works of Palestrina, Durante, Lotti, Pergolese, Gluck, Haydn, and Mozart such control is always present. Their music may be filled with expressions of grief and great pathos. But "the luminous sense of proportion never breaks down in extremes: everything finds its due place knit together in the whole; joy is never suffered to degenerate into unseemly uproar and even lamentation carries with it the most benign repose."[29]

We have been assuming that a musical sound is easily definable. But Hegel denies this. Not all sounds that are produced are musical. In fact, with the exception of the human voice, nothing in nature makes a musical sound.[30] Sculpture and painting find many of their ingredients among natural phenomena, for example, wood, stone, and colors. The basic materials of these arts are familiar even prior to their use in art work. On the other hand, man is solely responsible for the creation of the means whereby music is possible. Notes are not found in nature. They are produced by men and then formed into patterns. Similarly, cellos and trombones are made by men expressly to add sounds that are never to be found in a natural state. A musical sound, therefore, is one of the most ingenious occurrences that man has ever created. It is an immediate sign of man's inherent need to manifest the hidden creative urge that is within him.

We often overlook the fact that man is not simply a rational and featherless biped but that he is also a musical creature. Unlike any other animal, man is born with all the potentialities for being a magnificent musical instrument. The human voice "unites in itself the characteristics of both the wind instrument and the string. That is to say we have here in one aspect of it a column of air which vibrates, and, further, by virtue of the muscles, the principle of a string under tension."[31] Nor is this all. The human voice contains the only set of sounds that no instrument can surpass. Just as the color of human skin is "the most essentially perfect presentment of colour, so, too, we may affirm of the human voice that it contains the ideal compass of sound, all that in other instruments is differentiated in its several composite parts."[32] Furthermore, the cause of the sound emitted from a musical instrument is only indirectly due to human beings. The sound itself issues from something external to the musician. But the human voice exemplifies an immediate and direct transmission of all the emotions and moods that are taking place in the individual himself. "It is the human body itself from which the soul breaks into utterance."[33] For this reason the human voice is the best clue to a person's real personality. A rich inner life shows itself in the expressiveness of the voice. Undoubtedly, Hegel declared, this fact explains why the most beautiful voices are those of people of Italian descent. Their volatile temperaments require strong vocal cords.

Concluding his analysis of music, Hegel denied that he was being mystical by referring to a kind of gestalt unity in music. First of all, the sense of fusion and completion is obvious to anyone who has heard and appreciated music. Secondly, unity amidst diversity is to be found in our most basic perceptions.

When we perceive, for example, blue or yellow, green or red, in the specific purity of these colors, we receive in like manner the appearance of a perfectly simple determinacy, whereas violet readily is decomposed into its constituent colours of blue and red. Despite this fact the pure blue is not a simple fact, but a distinct correlation and fusion of light and shadow.[34]

Similarly, a set of actions can give us an immediate feeling of rightness or wrongness. However, music can only give us an abstract conception of unity. It gives us the emotion without specifying for us any content in which the emotion is necessarily involved. Only poetry gives us both unity and content.

VIII. THE ROMANTIC STAGE
OF ART: POETRY

To Hegel, poetry is the highest of all the arts. In it we have the realization of all those potentialities that can never be fully realized by the other arts. Unlike music, which stimulates emotions that do not explicitly refer to given ideas, poetry yields all the effects of music and adds concrete situations as well. In short, poetry "unites and embraces in a yet higher sphere, in the sphere of the very life of Spirit itself, the two extremes of the plastic arts and music."[1] Poetry, Hegel declared, "is capable of unfolding all the conditions of an event, a succession or interchange of emotional states, passions, conceptions, and the exclusive course of human action with more completeness than any other art."[2] Thus poetry, alone among the arts, can give an explicit image of mind and intelligence in action. There is no phase of human personality, no secret recess of human experience, that is not open to poetic inspection. Neither painting nor music is able to bring before us with such vividness the complexities of man insofar as he is a thinking and feeling being.

Nor is the fact that painting and sculpture are more successful in portraying the human figure a mark of deficiency in poetry. The purpose of art is not merely to provide us with an image of what appears. Rather its task is artfully to transform images so that the quality of the Idea is best revealed. Painting presents a unified whole and suggests some of the ideality present in human nature. But the greatness of man appears in his actions and in his conduct; painting can only very partially depict action and conduct. Poetry alone, by employing temporal sequence, is able to accomplish this. Everything has a "history, a change, sequence, and exclusive whole of varied conditions. And this is even more true of the sphere of spirit, which can only be exhaustively portrayed as veritable spirit in phenomenal guise when it is set before our imagination as such a process."[3] Poetry, therefore, can fuse together a series of events and show us a completed action from beginning to end. In all the other arts, prior and later events are inserted into the art work by the observer, but it is in poetry, especially the drama, that such events are explicitly given and fused into an organic whole.

It is true that poetry, like music, employs tone in order to convey its effects. But whereas in music tone is a crucial instrument for appealing to emotion, in poetry ideas and images play a more critical role. Thus in poetry melody and harmony lose the individuality that they attain in music. All that remains of such elements are certain general characteristics like "the generalized configuration of the time-measure of syllables and words, to which we may add euphony, rhythm, and the like."[4] It should be noted that poetry utilizes these characteristics not because they play an essential role, but because even the combination of words and sentences used by the poet must be given form and pattern. Art, Hegel declared, "cannot permit any mode of its external manifestation whatever to be entirely a question of accidental caprice."[5]

However, there is no necessity for the artist to impose any *specific* form. Some pattern is required, but it can be any one of an indefinite number. In fact, Hegel insists that a great poem can be translated into different languages and even transformed into prose without any real loss of value:

It is of no consequence whether a poetical work be read in private or listened to; and for the same reason it can also, without essential depreciation of value, be translated into other tongues, be transferred from versification into prose, and thereby transmitted in tonal relations of an entirely different character.[6]

What is important is the content of the poem, not its particular external form. This does not mean that the essence of the poem is simply one of conveying some general intellectual meaning, or merely describing ideal events. The artist shapes occurrences with his imagination, by means of which he fills in and completes what is only suggested in external events. For him the fragments of ideal action that appear in experience are molded into a unified whole in which the Idea is fully and explicitly realized. Events become transformed in his mind into an "organic whole, which in its parts presents the appearance of [an] . . . ideal synthesis."[7] And fortunately the poet has the one medium which is best able to express the most subtle actions and characterizations. Poetry, in Hegel's words, can be defined "as the *universal* art, which is capable of reclothing and expressing under every conceivable mode every content that can possibly enter into or proceed from the imagination of man."[8]

But this very limitlessness of poetic subject matter can lend itself to abuses. Just as music can become so abstract that it cannot be related to anything in human experience, so also poetry, with its emphasis on metaphor and subjectivity and its basis primarily in the subjective imaginative processes of the poet, is able to divorce itself from any attachment to the things and properties that are given in sense perception. The poetic art, Hegel stated, often "comes dangerously near to bidding goodbye to the region of sense altogether."[9] It is this danger that the poet must guard against. He must never use words and sentences in such a way that they are unable to arouse in the reader some form of meaningful imagery.

Since the poet has to complete and unify a series of events and actions, he should have a great knowledge of human psychology and sociology. He must know what motivates human beings and how they react under various conditions. He, more than anyone else, must be sensitive to the occurrence of those

incidents during which man's more idealistic and less animalistic tendencies come to the fore. By describing these incidents
and, with the help of imagination, giving them the kind of consummation that would best demonstrate their implicit ideality,
the poet visualizes for mankind what is valuable and significant
in human existence. For this reason, Hegel maintained, the
poet "has been the most universal and cosmopolitan instructor
of the human race and is so still."[10]

The knowledge that is communicated by poetry must not be
identified with the knowledge of the sciences. Even though the
prose language of the sciences sometimes approximates the
poetic language of poetry, still some fundamental distinctions
can be drawn between the information yielded by the sciences
and by poetry. Scientific knowledge is concerned with defining
nature as an entity independent of human emotions; poetry is
concerned with defining nature in its involvement in human
experience. The universals of science refer to particulars whose
subjective connotations have been deliberately and carefully
discarded. The universals of poetry refer to particulars chosen
deliberately and carefully for their subjective connotations.
Science may describe the processes of nature, but it ignores
the processes of experience.

The rare feelings of completion and consummation are only
incidental parts of scientific inquiry. But to the poet these
feelings are a primary source of interest and concentration.
His task becomes one of making explicit the universal forces
that permeate some of the events in which men are involved.
The poet is not therefore required to explain these forces.
Such laws are not explicitly given to him, nor does he attempt
to discern them in the way that a philosopher or a scientist
does. The poet is the truly sensitive observer. In an instant
he can sense where an action is beginning to develop, where
some rational but hidden process is beginning to actualize
itself. To the poet belongs the keen eye that recognizes the
event which is potentially significant for all men.

> [Poetry] is the *original* imaginative grasp of truth, a form of knowledge, which fails as yet to separate the universal from its living existence in the particular object, which does not as yet contrast law and phenomena, object and means, or relate the one to the other in subordination to the process of human reason, but comprehends the one exclusively in the other and by virtue of the other.[11]

The artist intuits that some actions and occurrences are suggestive of something out of the ordinary. He then nurtures this suggestion and brings it to fruition. His "mode of apprehending, reclothing and expressing fact is throughout one of construction."[12] An ordinary sentence is changed into a member of an emotion-laden experience in which there can be realization, frustration, and hope. Thus, there is a distich in Herodotus which refers to the slain heroes of Thermopylae. The words refer to a bare fact, but by forming the words into a distich rather than a sentence, the fact is made into a significant event; rather than being one fact among a myriad of others, it is made a part of a crucial human experience.[13] Thus the poet takes the facts and makes them live for us. He rejuvenates our impressions of things by giving them roles in a wider, more meaningful context. Ordinary consciousness, Hegel tells us, is primarily "a mere flux and contiguity of indifference."[14] But consciousness that can perceive in terms of poetic wholes, in which universal meanings are implicit, is an active and interested consciousness.

Analogously, ordinary usage of language is devoid of vivid impressions and images. In spite of the many metaphors and similes in our language, we usually speak with little, if any, recourse to imagery. The phrases "the sun" or "in the morning" are no doubt meaningful to us. But in our ordinary use of such terms there rarely comes to mind actual images of the sun or of the morning.[15] However, when Homer says, "When now the dawning Eos soared heavenwards with rosy fingers," an image immediately comes to mind accompanied by a feeling of anticipation of new events. The sentence "Alexander conquered the Persian empire" states a fact. but "it fails to image before us anything of the appearance and reality of the exploit accomplished by Alexander."[16] In essence, Hegel maintained, the poetic conception takes the significant fact and by the use of vivid imagery presents to us what this significance is.[17] It is in order to obtain the vividness, the significance, and the implications of the great event that Homer always chooses to use pictorial adjectives when he describes his heroes. Achilles is swift-footed; the Achaeans are bright-greaved; Hector is of the glancing helm; Agamemnon is the lord of peoples.

Hegel's concept of "creative totality" does not involve a mere combination of universal and particular. In the genuine poem or play the meaning is not added to the work as an extrinsic factor, nor are the incidents of a play or poem mere devices for demonstrating some objective moral or conception. Each part must be important in its own right. Otherwise the art work becomes no more than the mechanical realization of some inevitable end. The parts are robbed of "really free stability and thereby of every sort of vitality."[18] The actors become no more than pawns used as means for some external end. In the genuine art work "the organic completeness is equally asserted in subordinate detail, precisely as in the human organism every member, every finger is rounded with exquisite delicacy in its unified completeness, and as a rule, we find in Nature that every particular existence is enclosed within a perfect world of its own."[19] Nor is such a unity mystical, Hegel reiterated. In music, the dominant, the third, and the fifth are independent tones, each emitting its own individual sound. But played all together they give us the unity of the trichord.[20] Similarly, yellow, blue, red, and green are all different colors, but they still "maintain a harmony throughout."[21]

The organic unity in poetry is not found in any other kind of writing. Historical writing often seems to have a unity that is similar to that found in the poem and in the great tragedy. The historian often presents events in terms of a beginning that leads to some inevitable end. He depicts the rise and fall of various personalities. But the historian, if he is doing his job adequately, must take into account the chance factors that prohibit events from developing in some rational sequence. He is required to record how minor incidents can destroy personalities before they have fully realized their potentialities. In short, unlike the poet, he must permit events and human activity to appear "in all their objective contingency, dependence, and mysterious caprice."[22] Similarly, biographical writing has a sort of unity, but again this unity is never as organic as it is in the play. The biographer has to take into account many purely fortuitous actions. Unlike the poet, he cannot manipulate events in such a way that an individual's entire lifetime is revealed as a consistent unfolding and actualization of great and noble potentialities. Both the historian and the biographer are unable to present us with organically unified material, with a picture of a life that has developed successfully.

On the other hand, even though the poet must also rely on the facts of science and experience, he uses such material to create from his own resources, "as something newborn, that which, without such mediation, would have, in the plain and blunt particular case, wholly failed to impress us with the free spirit he communicates."[23] The poet brings to his material the power of vivid description as well as great sensitivity to those facts that have implicit in them a particular significance for men. For this reason Hegel believed that the best kind of poetry is written in old age. Only as a man matures and undergoes a great deal of experience does he obtain the sensitivity to events that are significant to men. It is to a blind old man, Homer, that we attribute the great Homeric epics. Goethe also realized his full genius only in old age.[24]

The constant endeavor to describe experience in such a way that it becomes significant to men leads poets to use metaphor, simile, and other figures of speech. Hegel approved of the use of such devices, but he warned that they are effective only insofar as they actually cause re-evaluations of what is being experienced. A metaphor is a technique for giving things of experience a meaning they did not have before. But when the same metaphor is repeatedly used the mind becomes inured to it in the same way that repeated use of drugs can gradually make the drug ineffective. Unfortunately, metaphors and similes, like other words and expressions, become incorporated into the language even after they have lost their capacity to stimulate the mind and recast facts. As a result, we still find poets who will use expressions which might have been refreshing and original at some earlier time, but which are now hackneyed.

In general, of course, poets seek to be very careful in their use of words. Sometimes, however, in their eagerness to describe an experience they use too many words and too much repetition. Unwittingly they fall into the same difficulty as does a musician who becomes so impressed by a given melody that he reiterates it until it becomes monotonous. The proliferation of similes, one piled on another, is very conspicuous in much of the Arabian, Persian, Spanish, and Italian literature.[25] Hence, we readily tire of them even though, like rich wine, they initially attract us. Nor were the Greek and Roman literatures free from unnecessary adornments. Virgil and Horace show a sense of restraint and care. But even in their work "we already feel that Art is to a real extent nothing but artifice, elaboration of effect on its own account."[26] Oddly enough, Hegel maintains that only Homer seems to be free of any extraneous verbiage; his language flows freely and naturally. We are never conscious of any straining for effect, of any interest in imagery and word music simply for their own sake.[27]

There is a further precaution the poet must take. Words, Hegel observed, are curious entities in that only rarely do they designate one and only one image. Every person attaches his own set of images to the expressions that he seriously uses. Thus there are some people who associate the most fantastic images with words. If the poet is unaware of the associations that are most often made he runs the risk of making statements which may not accomplish the effect he seeks.

Poets have introduced various techniques to control the elusiveness of words. Thus, by changing sentence structure they have sought to obtain a stricter control over meaning. By transforming the usual contexts in which specific terms occur, poets are able to divorce words from their everyday connotations. Hegel says that the language used by the poet should "not remain in the formless and undefined stream that we have in the immediate contingency of ordinary conversation."[28] The poet ought to use versification, rhythm, and the other techniques which are familiar to him in order to avoid the possible attachment to expressions which have loose and undesired meanings.

On the other hand, some of the greatest poems use very ordinary words and constructions. Indeed, the poetry of Homer is "barely distinguishable from ordinary speech."[29] But, first of all, Homer was writing at a time when the mere use of speech to express an imaginative idea was itself a great feat. His words were probably very unusual to his readers. We are long since accustomed to using language as a means of communicating abstract and imaginative pictures. But in Homer's time such familiarity was lacking.

Furthermore, Homer's language is not really ordinary speech since each phrase is deliberately purged of those elements which could make the Homeric hero an ordinary individual. Each word in itself is indeed very simple. But, when placed in the grammatical constructions which Homer uses, the words no longer have the usual connotations.

Some poets, such as Lessing, Schiller, and Goethe, attempted, especially in tragedy, to introduce ordinary speech, but they were unsuccessful. Thus, in his *Nathan*, Lessing returned to the use of iambic verse. In his *Don Carlos*, Schiller also returned to verse. Goethe was so dissatisfied with his earlier prose treatment of *Iphigenia* and *Tasso* that he later transformed them into verse.[30] Thus the artist, if he is to obtain the effect he seeks, cannot rely upon the way language is used in everyday affairs.

Although mere sound effect for its own sake is a detriment to good poetry, this does not mean that the poet can neglect the sounds of words and phrases. Very often the sounds produced can succeed in distracting us from the meanings they were intended to convey. Instead of seeking to partake of the experience the writer is presenting to us, we are repelled by the irregularity or faultiness of the rhythm, or by the raucousness of the sound. Thus, in Sanscrit, Greek, or Latin, if two or more consonants are placed between two vowels, the relation constitutes "a difficult transition in speech."[31] The same harsh effect frequently occurs in modern languages. Some series of sounds make us stumble or become more conscious of the form rather than the meaning of the expression. Of course, sometimes such irregularities are deliberately used by the poet in order to detroy possible monotony. Hegel emphasizes that monotony is the worst enemy of the poet. Such specialized sound patterns as those exemplified by the elegy, the strophe, the lyric, and the chorus are designed to make the mind more alert to the action that is unfolding. Each device acts as a means of emphasizing the attitude or mood that is to prevail when a given action is developing. The hexameter, for example, "in the tranquil wave of its forward stream, is particularly adapted to the even flow of epic narration."[32] The iambic "moves forward with rapidity, and as such is peculiarly suitable to dramatic dialogue."[33] The anapest "indicates the clear-slipping march of joyful exultation."[34] But when the poet deviates from these tried and tested methods, he runs the risk of making the form a barrier to the meaning.

Rhythm and rhyme are two of the most important techniques that the poet employs. Their function, Hegel stated, is simply to call attention to the fact that a special kind of experience is being described. Like the beat in music, both rhythm and rhyme are meant to make explicit the sense of time coming and passing.[35] They operate as signs that language is being used to communicate highly significant experiences rather than mere information. For these reasons Christianity has made extensive use of both rhythm and rhyme. The kind of experience which the Christian wishes to communicate requires a language that can provoke man's profoundest emotions. Thus, St. Ambrose' hymn to the Holy Spirit breaks into rhyme. St. Augustine's first work against the Donatists is also in rhymed song.

Turning now to the various kinds of poetry, Hegel lists what he believes to be the three most important types, namely, *epic* poetry, in which an ideal objective action is depicted while the poet himself remains unobtrusively in the background; *lyrical* poetry, in which the poet's own feelings and desires permeate the actions that are being described; and *dramatic* poetry, which combines the features of epic and lyrical poetry. The drama describes a completed action in which human emotions and conflicts are explicitly revealed and utilized in order to further the development of the action. Hegel now undertakes a detailed analysis of these three highest art forms of the Romantic Age.

The epic form of poetry is, according to Hegel, one of man's greatest attempts to describe those events and actions which attain major social significance. In a very important sense the epic celebrates those instances in which men exemplify the ideals held by a given society.

The attempt to celebrate important events by means of art, however, does not begin with the epic. At the very earliest period of man's existence some effort is made to immortalize deeds that the group considered important. Some primitive form of either painting or sculpture is used. But with the arrival of language men had an instrument which could fully satiate the desire to pay homage to the ideal moments that sometimes appeared.

At first only crude and very simple uses are made of the possibilities inherent in language. Thus the epigram represents one of the very earliest endeavors to employ words in such a way that a value-laden experience is presented. The ancient gnomes and elegies are also very early attempts to glorify man's significant adventures. They are somewhat more successful than the epigram in emphasizing "what is of sterling validity, whether as the object of human obligation or the sense of honour and propriety."[36] As these early forms of poetry develop, new insights into the plasticity and other remarkable capabilities of language become utilized until, finally, the works of Homer and Hesiod appear. However, even such a significant work as Hesiod's *Theogony* suggests but does not give us the essential mark of an epic—the description of a unified event. It does not present to us "an essentially *complete whole*."[37]

The organic unity of the epic must be sharply distinguished from that found in the lyric and the drama. The action of the epic emphasizes man's social, human, and political needs rather than his spiritual aspirations. It describes an action in which all the highest ideals of a society are displayed. By the use of a single organically unified event a glimpse is obtained of all the values that permeate a given culture. Thus, to quote Hegel, "the collective world-outlook and objective presence of a national spirit, displayed as an actual event in the form of its self-manifestation, constitutes, and nothing short of this does so, the content and form of the true epic."[38]

Epics, therefore, are descriptions of a selected series of occurrences in which the highest social values are given concrete representation. Each actor in the event becomes an instrument for displaying a behavior pattern or relationship which will signify heroic qualities. For this reason biblical literature abounds with epic episodes. Many of the incidents related are designed to reflect the ideals and hopes of a given society or people. But the Bible as a whole cannot be considered an epic. The Bible, including both the Old and New Testaments, is primarily a history. It is organized chronologically rather than organically. In some of the incidents there is development from a beginning to an end, but this does not characterize the

entire Bible.[39] "The whole is not a work of art."[40] The holy
book of the Moslems, the Koran, is also not an epic. Even
though it represents the values of a people it does not display
these values in a concrete evolving event. It is neither organically unified nor does it "offer us a mirror of the national spirit
in all its compass."[41]

On the other hand, the *Iliad* and the *Odyssey*, as well as, to
a lesser extent, the Indian *Ramayana* and *Mahabharata*, are
excellent examples of genuine epics. The Homeric epics, especially, give us an all-inclusive picture of the ideals held by the
Greeks. Every level of Greek society is inspected and described.
In Hegel's view, the *Odyssey* "not only brings us into contact
with the domestic life of the Greek chieftains, their servants
and subordinates, but also unfolds the richest variety with its
tales of the many opinions of foreign peoples, the hazards of
sea-life, the dwellings of distant lands, and so forth."[42] Similarly, in the *Iliad* we are given a view of "the entire compass of
terrestrial existence, no less than human life, in marriages,
judicial affairs, agriculture, the might of armies, the private
wars of cities, and much else."[43]

The concrete imagery is an important feature of the epic.
Without it we are left either with an amorphous abstraction or
a strict moral treatise. In fact, the lack of concrete imagery is
the reason neither the *Divine Comedy* nor the *Nibelungenlied* can legitimately be called epics. Dante's work, according
to Hegel, is more a moral sermon—although a very good
sermon—than a presentation of concrete scenes in which the
ideals of the medieval age are revealed. Dante's angels and
devils "inhabit no truly positive world open to our detailed
approach; it exists solely as instrumental to the final fruition
or due punishment of mankind."[44] Similarly, the *Nibelungenlied* reveals a complete absence of "any definite realization of
a visible world or environment, so that the narrative tends in
this respect to assume the strain or tone of the mere ballad-
singer."[45]

Hegel pointed out an interesting fact about epics, that they can deal only with specific kinds of societies. The epic obtains its interest by describing peoples and groups in which laws and regulations are not yet formally prescribed. Thus the Greek society described by Homer is not yet fully organized. There are no specific written laws dealing with what can or cannot be done by members of the group. Morality is in the process of being formulated; there are no specific statements of right and wrong as we know them today. The Greek heroes do not exemplify moral views that have already been adequately stated, but rather views that will take hundreds of years to explicate. They signify the initial stages of a society. For this reason it is not too difficult to understand the fascination that the epic hero has for us. He signifies for us the personification of ethical action. In him we see abstract ethical theory translated into concrete practice. He acts as we would want to act if there were more worlds to conquer and new societies to build. But, unfortunately for us, Hegel thought, there are no longer any worlds to conquer and societies to build. Our moral codes have already been made explicit. We live in groups rigidly controlled by numerous social rules. Hence the poet of today cannot write epics. His characters cannot have the freedom and spontaneity of an Odysseus. They must, on the contrary, be primarily products of an environment that demands their full obedience. The poet's heroes "are now confronted with material obligations rather as a necessary force external to themselves than one which their own inner life asserts, and which it compels them to substantiate as its fulfillment."[46]

Thus, law has finally become more an external than an internal force. There are no longer individuals who exemplify and fight for hidden sets of moral principles. The principles have now been discovered and accepted. The poet, therefore, must look for other avenues that are not yet closed. Somewhere there must be a type of freedom and idealism which is analogous to that found in Greek society.

One of the most interesting prophecies Hegel made is his

prediction that this new avenue will present itself in the psychological, as distinct from the behavioristic, aspect of man. Personality and emotion will become the most important subject matter for the poet. In the kind of closed society that prevails today, Hegel argued, "the individual life will seek in part to find expression in an equally independent world and growth of personal vision, reflection, and emotion, which are not carried further into the sphere of action."[47]

Although epics deal with the earliest phases of civilization, they are not necessarily written during these early periods. Homer wrote his poems centuries later than the Trojan War. But the poet must at least have some awareness of the kind of freedom and self-expression that early societies possessed. He cannot be so restricted by social, political, and economic regulations that a less enclosed civilization is almost inconceivable to him. Homer himself lived in a Greek society that was probably not yet fully formed. Although it was undoubtedly not as primitive as the civilization described in the *Odyssey*, it was still not too far removed from the Odyssean civilization. Homer's society had not stifled his capacity to free himself from his own cultural milieu and then completely absorb himself in the background of the Homeric epics.[48] But contemporary poets have difficulty writing epics. Too much time has passed; too many restrictions have been imposed. It is difficult for us to conceive of a social group in which government and law are not so completely defined as they are today. We are so much products of our environment that our views are constantly being saturated by beliefs and considerations which would be detrimental to an understanding of the social system defined by Homer.

But if we are so far removed from Homeric society, why are we so interested in it and why is Homer today considered one of the truly great writers? Hegel answered that the epics sustain interest because, first of all, they present us with a glorified image of what we believe to be heroic and ideal. Secondly, they deal with perennial issues and struggles among human beings. Anyone who has felt the desire to realize something better in himself, to make both his realities and ideals identical, lives vicariously in the scenes and events in which the hero participates. He finds in the epic hero the actualization of potentialities which any rational being would like to realize, and which, in a metaphysical sense, signifies the manifestation of God in man. Homer, therefore, has a universal message. "The superb directness with which he deals with matters of divine or ethical import, the nobility of the characters and of everything living therein embraced, the pictorial quality of their presentment to the reader, all this insures an undying truth for succeeding ages."[49] Similarly, the epic passages of the Old Testament have endured from the earliest time to the present because they describe actions that can have inspirational meaning to all thinking readers. On the other hand, some works cannot stand the test of time. The *Nibelungenlied*, with its exploits of Siegfried, is "for present consciousness a state of things wholly gone forever, swept away once and for all with a besom."[50] In the *Ramayana*, also, there are strong traces of provincialism. The character of the Hindu race is presented as such a unique type that "the essential features of our common humanity are unable to assert themselves through the veil of national idiosyncrasy."[51]

The greatest epics, therefore, incorporate actions and situations that are significant to all individuals who have ever concerned themselves with the question of how a human being ought to behave. Hegel now endeavors to define in greater detail the kind of actions and situations that are proper for the genuine epic.

It is clear from what has been said before that the epic action can be displayed only at an early stage in the development of society. During this early period there are no laws of social order, that is, *written* laws. "Rather it is the *intuitive* sense of right and fairness, the moral habit, the temperament, the personality, which supply the support, as they are the source, of such a social order."[52] Each individual is in himself a source of morality. Thus the relation between Agamemnon and the other chieftains is not a defined relation between a king and his vassals. He, as well as each of the other chieftains, is a definite individual demanding recognition of his own rights and freely asserting either approval or disapproval. Achilles always has the right to agree or disagree with any of Agamemnon's decisions. And when he refrains from battle because he disagrees with Agamemnon's judgment, he is perfectly within his rights. This kind of individuality also appears in the *Cid* as well as the epics of Ossian, Ariosto, and Tasso. The hero, therefore, in spite of the moral principle he incorporates, is not strictly determined by any set of principles. Nor can he be controlled against his will by any other person. He is a genuinely free individual.

Furthermore, the heroic personality thrives under conditions of conflict and collision. By means of collisions, situations are created in which his potentiality for ideal action can be realized. For this reason war is a good subject matter for the epic poet since it is in war, the greatest kind of collision, that ideal action has the best opportunity to appear. But the war treated by the epic poet ought to be one between different cultures rather than one which is internal to a culture. Civil wars involve more personal and emotional factors than wars between cultural or national groups. The former is best treated in tragedy, where the collisions that involve intimate and personal emotions can be more adequately described. In both Aeschylus and Shakespeare, for example, civil wars play a much more significant role than wars between nations.

Nevertheless, the epic poet cannot use any war between nations as his subject matter. In the epic we are not simply dealing with the triumph of good over evil. Even though such a triumph is extremely important to men and they enjoy its appearance in art, it does not signify the important aspect of the epic. The kind of triumph the epic poet is seeking to portray is one in which a new form of the good has evolved. He deals with those collisions in which the various opposing forces have their share of justice and virtue. Then, when the collision is finally resolved, a new, more profound sense of justice and virtue has made its appearance. Thus, the Trojans are not evil men fighting against good men, the Greeks. Both sides have strong, brave, and highly moral soldiers. And when the Trojans lose we do not conclude that good has triumphed over evil. On the contrary, we recognize that the struggle has led to the birth of a new world which will regard the feats of both the Trojans and the Greeks as exemplars of the idealism and self-lessness that men sometimes possess.

Hence the collision the epic poet seeks is one in which the resultant resolution will lead to a greater moral awakening than ever before.

> In all the greatest Epopees we find nations which differ from each other in moral customs, religion, and language, in a word, in all that concerns their spiritual and external life, brought into collision; and we are ready to contemplate such [conflicts] without any revulsion on account of the triumph we find asserted there of a nobler principle of world-evolution over a less exalted [one], a victory assured by a bravery that is simply annihilating.[53]

Curiously enough, Hegel did not believe that such conflicts could ever again occur in Europe. In Europe "every nation finds itself conditioned by its neighbor, and cannot venture on its own account to wage any war with another European nation."[54] He admitted, however, that the seeds of a possible epic subject matter might be in the making. Perhaps some day the epic poet may again have a subject matter in "the portrayal of the victory of some future and intensely vital rationality of the American nation over the prison-house of the spirit which forever pursues its monotonous task of self-adjustment and particularization."[55]

Even though the epic poet looks to the world for the models which he can use for presenting the epic action, we should not think of him as a mere chronicler of a significant historical event. Most significant events have an infinite number of implications and consequences which neither the historian nor the epic writer can ever really describe. Just as the sculptor molds the crude clay into a highly finished product, so also the epic poet is required to mold an event until all incidents extraneous to it are eliminated. In actual life crucial events are intermeshed with irrelevant and unimportant incidents. Furthermore, in actual life an event is rarely organized and planned perfectly. The greatest battle is usually filled with miscalculations and blatant blunders. The epic poet has the task of erasing the disorderly elements and emphasizing the orderliness and organic unity of the event. Even when such unity is not completely given, he is required to use his imagination to fill in the deficiencies. Usually the poet accomplishes this task by considering what conditions ought to be present if the hero is to be able to perform significant and idealistic actions. Incidents, then, are included or excluded by virtue of their causal connection with the final consummation in which the hero performs the great action. The *Cid* clearly exemplifies this procedure. And in the *Iliad* and the *Odyssey* we see how the poet has deliberately created incident after incident which can be used to display the qualities of Achilles or Odysseus.

These incidents are not used simply to display the hero's strength and courage. They also become a means of signifying a "complete" man, that is, a man who can become a national symbol of all the various ideals held by a people. Both Achilles and Odysseus are strong and courageous, but they are also wise and cunning, practical and far-seeing. They represent, Hegel maintained, "in a typical way, national opinion and its active pursuits."[56] The nation is, as it were, "focussed as a single living soul in them, and as such they fight out its main enterprise."[57] Thus Achilles combines in himself all those qualities that the Greeks idealized and strove to attain. Odysseus mirrors the qualities that the Greeks believed should characterize the returning hero.

We can note that the same kind of idealization occurs in the tragedy as well. But whereas the epic deals with such idealization in terms of events of national importance, the tragedy is confined to idealization amidst personal relationships. As a result, destiny plays a much more important role in epics than in tragedies. In the tragedy, destiny is more hypothetical. If the hero acts in a given way then certain consequences will follow. The consequences are contingent on the actions of the hero. On the other hand, in the epic destiny has a more inevitable character. Even though the hero can make choices, there are certain inevitable ends which he can never change. The epic moves "within the element itself of essentially necessary existence. Therefore, the individual has no choice but to follow this particular substantive condition; and, in its process of being, to adapt himself to it or not, and then to suffer as he is able and is forced to suffer."[58]

However, destiny need not be presented in such a way that individuals are no more than mere pawns. In some epics destiny does play such an important role that the individuality of the characters is blotted out. This occurs in the *Nibelungenlied,* where the sense of destiny is so overwhelming that the characters can only be regarded as puppets rather than free men. A great deal of Christian literature has the same basic flaw. The various attempts at creating Christian epics suffer from too much abstractness. "The variously personified powers, passions, genii, angels, and so forth, that we meet with in Christendom possess for the most part too little individual independence, and consequently tend only to affect us in a cold and abstract sort of way."[59] But in the Greek epics there is an excellent blending of fate and freedom. The gods, as well as men, retain their individuality and freedom. This is accomplished by a distinction that is made between the inevitability of a given end and the freedom with which it is reached. Achilles is destined to die in a certain way, but he is still an individual who becomes angry, fights, and reveals personal animosities. Odysseus must inevitably return to his homeland, but this does not make him any less a free man in his personal behavior. The gods determine the end of a man, but they give him the right to develop his own personal traits and they give him the conditions under which his character can reveal itself.[60]

Obtaining the proper balance of fate and freedom is no easy matter for the epic poet. Too much emphasis on fate makes the hero a mere puppet and, therefore, his heroic qualities are lessened. After all, anyone can win a battle if the gods guarantee it. On the other hand, too much emphasis on freedom makes the hero too human, and then we question his right to be an exemplar of moral virtue.

Homer's genius was sufficient to find exactly the right proportion. But many other poets who have attempted to write epics have failed. Virgil has often been compared to Homer, but Hegel believed that this comparison is unflattering to Virgil. First of all, there are very obvious flaws in the *Aeneid*. Virgil never permits his characters to speak as they probably would have during the early phases of society. This does not mean that their speech ought to have a primitive quality. But it ought not to be so completely Romanized that we become immediately aware of an anachronism. But more important, Virgil's gods and heroes never have the spontaneity of Homer's creations. They are like puppets utilized by the poet to glorify the Roman Empire. Also, they have been made so prosaic and ordinary that they have lost their god-like character and become average human beings. In Homer, on the other hand, "the gods are wafted in a magical light between poetry and reality: they are not permitted to approach the imagination so nearly that the apparition of them confronts us with all the detail of ordinary life; nor are they left so undefined that they lose all appearance of vital reality as we look at them."[61]

The difference between Virgil and Homer is even more evident when we compare their treatment of similar scenes. The Dido scene has been universally acclaimed. But it does not compare to the simplicity and truth found in the Homeric narratives of Circe and Calypso.[62] Aeneas' descent into the Underworld seems almost pedestrian when compared with the descent made by Odysseus. Odysseus does not simply descend a flight of steps in order to enter Hades. Homer is so much aware of Greek mythology and ritual that he recognizes the importance of describing the ceremony required before one can enter Hades. Virgil, on the other hand, does not attribute any such significance to the mythology and ritual of early society.

For very similar reasons other endeavors at epic writing have failed. The same artificiality, Hegel maintained, appears in such works as Milton's *Paradise Lost*, Bodmer's *Noachid*, Klopstock's *Messias,* and Voltaire's *Henriade.* In all these works "we cannot fail to detect a real cleft between the content and the reflection of the poet which modifies his description of the events, characters, and circumstances."[63] In Milton "we find emotions and observations obviously the growth of an imagination and ethical ideas inseparable from his own age."[64] In Klopstock "we have God the Father, the history of Jesus Christ, patriarchs and angels combined with our German education of the eighteenth century, and the ideas of Wölffian metaphysic."[65] These poets, by bringing into their work their own contemporary values, diminish the effectiveness of their poems. They forget that the values in the genuine epic must be such that they are universal in scope and not solely products of a given society at a given time.

The epic poem concentrates more on the actual behavior than on the psychological feelings of the individuals involved in the heroic action. For this reason there is little, if any lyrical poetry to be found in the epic. The lyric, for Hegel, is the best vehicle for expressing strong emotions. But the epic uses other means in order to describe scenes which involve highly emotional situations. Primarily, the language makes little reference to the introspective and psychological. Rather the terminology refers to the external cause of the emotion. The hero does not bemoan his fate; he does not express his fears and frustrations. He points to, and stoically accepts, the conditions that have resulted in his misfortune.

Thus, the lament of Hecuba over Hector, or Achilles over the death of Patroclus, or the parting of Hector and Andromache—episodes which could easily be treated in a lyric vein—are "held throughout within the epic temper."[66] The emotional impact of these scenes is not derived from language which refers to the personal feelings of the individuals concerned. On the contrary, the language designates objective events. The scene between Hector and Andromache—a scene which Hegel believes "belongs unquestionably to one of the finest conceivable efforts of epic poetry"[67]—especially exemplifies the manner in which emotive and introspective language is excluded from the epic form. In a detailed analysis of the discourse between Hector and Andromache, Hegel endeavors to show how emotion is displayed in the epic. Unlike lyrical poetry, in which the explicit formulation of the poet's emotions is used to arouse the reader's emotions, epic poetry permits objective events themselves to obtain the reader's response. For example, Hector's words to his wife when he considers the possibilities of her capture by the Greeks are pathetic and full of feeling, yet the emotion is never directed toward himself.

> All that Hector says here is full of feeling, pathetic enough, yet . . . in the epic vein, inasmuch as the picture which he outlines of suffering, and which brings pain to himself, in the first place depicts circumstantially objective conditions as such, and in the second place because all that affects and moves him does not appear as personal volition, or individual resolve, but rather as a necessity which is not at the same time his own aim and will.[68]

But consider the battlefield scene in Schiller's *Maid of Orleans,* involving Joan of Arc and the English knight, Montgomery. In the moment of danger he contemplates his own possible death and pities himself for having to die in a foreign land.

With the development of civilization, with its explicit statement of law and mores, the epic quality of poetry tends to diminish. The creation and acceptance of national states as natural units of society cause poets to look elsewhere for the subject matter that can produce the aesthetic response. Since the external social environment has attained stability, the fascination in depicting the creation of a national state and a national culture is no longer present. As a result, the poet begins to concentrate more on his own internal moods than on the occurrences in his social environment. When this new outlook appears, lyrical poetry begins to develop.

In the epic poem the subjective aspect of the poet remains essentially divorced from the content of his work. Homer himself so rarely appears in his epics that people sometimes claim he never existed. On the other hand, in lyric poetry the artist attempts "to unfold the content and activity of the personal life rather than the actual presence of the external fact."[69] The heroes of the Homeric epics will always remain vividly sketched before us. But in the lyric poetry of Pindar the heroes "are for us little better than empty names."[70] Only Pindar himself "remains before us immortal as the poet."[71]

The lyric poet, therefore, deals with the expression of personal emotion. "The most fleeting moods of the moment, the overjoyment of the heart, the swiftly passing gleams or clouds of careless merriment and jest, sorrow, melancholy, and complaint, in a word, all and every phase of emotion are here seized in their momentary movement or isolated occurrence, and rendered permanent in their expression."[72] Horace, for example, frequently stops and describes in detail some specific feeling he may have about a given event. For this reason important events are not necessarily excluded from lyrical treatment. In fact, much lyrical poetry deals with epic subject matter. Heroic songs, romances, and ballads can be concerned with national qualities and problems. But at the same time the treatment is lyrical in that the poet actively asserts himself and his viewpoint. The ballads of Goethe and Schiller as well as the Pindaric odes exemplify the use of epic material with lyrical treatment. The chosen event is combined with personal reflections on the part of the poet. In some of his odes Horace seems to say, "I will as myself, a man of culture and fame, write a poem on this subject."[73]

Hegel noted that the unrestricted use of emotion in the lyric lends itself to abuse. First of all, an expression of emotion can sometimes become pure sentimentalism if the poet is not careful. Even though the lyric deals with highly emotional situations, there must always be a sense of control. The emotion must be given to us in such a way that we are not embarrassed (or disgusted) by its presentation. Secondly, the poet sometimes has the mistaken belief that his personal reflections about himself and his moods must necessarily be of interest to the rest of the world. But this, of course, is false. The lyric must express emotions which the reader can share. For this reason genuine lyrics are generally more than mere outbursts of emotion. The poet projects himself into the external world and writes of his actions in and reactions to scenes that would be entertaining to the world at large. In the odes of Anacreon the poet describes his feelings and his actions as he drinks and dances among roses and fair maidens. Similarly, Goethe's songs incorporate scenes that are colorful and romantic.

In Hegel's view, the fact that most lyrics do allude to specific scenes and events does not vouch for the truth or falsity of those particular occurrences. The lyric poet can either accept reality or reject it. He may seek to express some great philosophical truths in order "to make them perceptible to sensuous apprehension."[74] On the other hand, the lyric often "does violence both to art and abstract thought."[75] Reality becomes absorbed in "personal feeling, vision, imagination, and thought."[76] The lyric poet has the freedom to utilize any subject and any theme from the most highly religious kind expressed in the Psalms of the Old Testament to the most insignificant kind often found in Horace and Klopstock. What engages his effort is not the definition of truth but rather "the process in virtue of which he exalts what is on its own account insignificant, either in external facts or petty occurrences, to the height of the emotion and idea they excite in himself."[77] The ideal lyric, however, combines intellectual content with genuine feeling. In this respect Schiller, Goethe, and Klopstock are the real masters. In them we find the kind of mastery that lyric poetry requires. Not only do they have a sensitivity to and understanding of human emotion, but they are also skilled in the use of such techniques as alliteration, rhyme, assonance, and rhythm. They also have an excellent understanding of the nature of music and, as a result, have a greater awareness of how sound operates and what combinations of sound can produce the emotion that is sought.[78]

The lyric is an important form of poetry, but in a sense it is the antithesis of epic poetry. It makes poetry more personal and more intimate but it also loses the concreteness and reality orientation of the epic. The drama is the synthesis of lyric and epic poetry. It combines the best elements in both art forms and produces a poetry that indicates man's highest endeavor to uncover all that is ideal in human existence. The drama more than any other art form can finally convey to us how the Idea, the Absolute, makes its appearance among human beings.

Dramatic action deals with the most complicated and yet the most important action in which human beings can participate. Sometimes men become engaged in collisions which demand the full use of their highest potentialities. Their physical as well as their rational powers are put to the highest test. Such collisions become the material which the dramatist uses in order to create his art.

As we have seen in the discussion of action in Chapter II, collisions must be of a certain sort before they can become the subject matter for great dramatic talent. First, the collision must be more than a simple struggle of good against evil. The opposing sides must have standards of truth and justice. Otherwise we obtain a purely moral rather than an aesthetic effect from the work. Secondly, the collisions must undergo development. We must be constantly aware that there is some highly significant effect which the action is seeking to produce, but this effect must not be thought of as some predetermined end which the actors are unable to avoid. The consummation must be regarded as a resultant of human activity causing plausible consequences which themselves make the final step all the more probable. Thus the unity of the tragedy "depends throughout on conditions of collision, human passion and characters, and leads therefore to actions and reactions, which in their turn call for some further resolution of conflict and disruption."[79]

Even though the dramatist must control the avenues that the actions can take, he must avoid making the actors mere puppets who are expected to respond mechanically to appropriate stimuli. Men are not actually men unless they are presented as beings who can err, make choices, and give vent to their own personalities.[80]

Personality, therefore, is a second important aspect of the drama. In the epic the traits that can become national symbols are frequently emphasized at the expense of the personal, purely private features that make a man a particular unique being. In the drama a specific unique man is placed in a conflict which does not simply threaten him with death but with the destruction of his whole set of values and beliefs. Odysseus may be in constant physical danger, but neither he himself nor anyone else threatens the validity of the moral code he accepts and acts upon.

On the other hand, the most fundamental beliefs of Orestes, Antigone, and Oedipus are constantly being challenged. These characters fascinate us because the struggles in which they are engaged can potentially result in much more than physical death. Orestes must decide whether he can actually kill his own mother and still live as a person. Antigone must decide whether to choose in favor of the laws of the state or her religious beliefs. Oedipus must determine how he can make his sin compatible with his own basic innocence. In each instance the conflict involves dilemmas that touch upon men's most basic attitudes and beliefs.

The dramatist makes these curiously paradoxical personal

conflicts his primary subject matter. In resolving them he chooses among several alternatives. Sometimes, as in the case of Antigone, the resolution consists in the destruction of both sides. Antigone is put to death, and Creon also is punished when his son and wife commit suicide.[81] At other times the resolution is more profound. Thus, in the *Oresteia* a reconciliation is made between Orestes and the Furies. In order that the life of Athens may continue to grow and to maintain its unity, the values upheld by Orestes and the Furies result in moral conflicts which must be adjudicated. Otherwise the very existence of society itself is threatened. This need to preserve the state explains the final decision reached by the Areopagus and Athene. Crucial conflicts must be mediated.

> The votes of the Areopagus are equal on either side. It is Athene, the goddess, the life of Athens, that is, imagined in its essential unity, who adds the white pebble, who frees Orestes, and at the same time promises altars and a cult to the Eumenides no less than Apollo.[82]

However, probably the most profound kind of resolution appears in the Oedipus tragedy. Here the resolution is primarily internal. In death Oedipus finds the resolution to his own internal struggle. A higher more inclusive law is seen to make his sin forgivable. But Hegel warned that Oedipus' sudden illumination must not be equated with the Christian view of the sinner whom God receives into His grace. "The illumination of Oedipus, on the contrary, remains throughout, in consonance with ancient ideas."[83] Even in the Greek period there was recognition that the ethical struggles of men were resolved in the next life.

We should note that even though the drama often deals with the relation of man to the gods, the conflicts are much more familiar to us than those presented in the epic. We are interested in the epic in spite of the fact that the situations presented are largely foreign to our experience. We are strongly impressed by the actions of glorified human beings engaged in cataclysmic collisions. But in the drama the collisions touch upon the situations that we do actually encounter. The depiction of the dramatic hero with his hopes and fears, his failures and successes, is closer to the experience in which we ourselves are involved. This does not imply that the drama deals with matters that are less important than those found in the epic. Dramatic action can and often does relate to the gods, the eternal forces, and divine ethical rights. But in the drama the gods are not

> saved from all action, as some serene figures of sculpture self-absorbed in a state of blessedness. What we have here [in the drama] is the divine in its community, as content, that is, and object of human personality, as concrete existence in its realization, invited to act and charged with movement.[84]

Because the dramatist is deeply concerned with such concrete matters, he must necessarily have an excellent knowledge of how human beings are motivated and how they will react under various conditions. It should be within his power to recognize "the ideal and universal substance which is at the root of human ends, conflicts, and destinies . . . the contradictions and developments which the particular action will, under the proposed conditions, necessarily involve and display . . . the rightful claim, no less than the wrongful misuse of the passions, which storm through the human heart and excite to action."[85] Furthermore, he must have a sense of the order that is often implicit in what to ordinary vision is "the ascendancy of obscurity, chance, and confusion."[86] In short, the dramatic poet "must in the profoundest sense make himself master of the essential significance of human action and the divine order of the world, and along with this of a power to unfold this eternal and essential foundation of all human characters, passions, and destinies in its clarity as also in its vital truth."[87] This super-knowledge that the poet requires makes him more than a mere mouthpiece of his age. In many cases his knowledge brings him into direct opposition to the ideas of his age and nation. In such instances, Hegel declared, "The responsibility for such a disunion does not rest with himself, but is a burden the public ought to carry. He has the single obligation to follow the lead of truth and his own compelling genius."[88]

The unity of the dramatic action is more compact than the unity of epic action. Change of place is as permissible in the drama as it is in the epic.[89] However, Hegel agreed that too many changes of place in the drama could cause disunity. The constant shifting of scenes can cause a strain on the imaginative faculty which keeps us aware at the present moment of what happened previously. In many of his tragedies and comedies Shakespeare tried to overcome the confusion resulting from too many changes in scene by posting notices which indicated the place the spectator was viewing. The most convenient course in such matters, Hegel concluded rather speciously, is to look for "a happy mean."[90] The scenes must not be so many that it becomes exceedingly difficult to produce a sense of developing action. At the same time they must not be so sparse that the imagination is overtaxed.

The time limit of the drama is also adjustable. If the action lacks serious import, if the collision does not require intense character development, then the time should be short. On the other hand, if the growth as well as the understanding of the action demands numerous situations which will present various facets of the main characters, "then the formal unity of a purely relative and entirely conventional duration of time will be essentially impossible."[91] The very process of unraveling complicated personality traits requires different time sequences.

Of course, the final determinant of how much time and how many scenes must be used is the action itself. Dramatic action, Hegel reiterated, is a sequence which can be taken in by an observer in such a way that the beginning is never forgotten. The time is never so long that the mind is taxed to remember what has already passed. Hegel would undoubtedly have approved of the views of contemporary aestheticians who have

expounded the notion of "psychic distance."[92] Just as we must
be the exact distance away from a painting in order to take in
its organic unity, so also the play must have the exact proportions which the intelligent mind can grasp as a unified whole.
No individual, no situation, must be extraneous. Hence, as
Hegel points out, in *Romeo and Juliet,* Shakespeare not only
resolves the difficulties between the two young lovers; he also
resolves the discord between the two families. Similarly, in
Hamlet the fortunes of Denmark are subsidiary to the main
interest. But Shakespeare settles those fortunes satisfactorily
by introducing Fortinbras. No issue is left undetermined.[93]

Hegel believed that the resolutions of conflicts can best be
accomplished in three acts. The first act initiates the action;
the second act develops it; the third act brings it to its consummation. Hegel was aware that it is always difficult to define
the exact beginning of an action. Nevertheless, since he believed that events were like animate objects, he argued that if
a given event takes place under certain conditions, then a
future event will necessarily occur. The acorn has in it the
essence to become an oak. Analogously, the beginning of the
dramatic event will be that event whose occurrence under
certain conditions will lead to a given consummation. "The
right point of departure will lie in the situation, out of which
the future evolution of that conflict, despite the fact that it
has not as yet broken out, will none the less issue in its further
course."[94]

As the action develops, the full significance and inevitability
of the conclusion is gradually revealed even to the actors
themselves. Thus Orestes gradually becomes fully aware of
the terrible deed he must perform. With this realization the
emotion of *pathos* enters into the tragedy. Pathos, for Hegel,
is the emotion that occurs when suddenly there is an explicit
awareness of how duty can cause the destruction of love and
happiness.[95] We sympathize with Orestes because we recognize
that he is a man who is morally committed to accomplishing

an act which he himself finds horrible to contemplate. We pity Orestes because his conflict cannot be resolved without dire consequences to his own moral beliefs. In short, for Hegel, pathos is that emotion we feel upon viewing a rational and intelligible course of action that, unfortunately, leads to human disaster. For this reason the gods can never be said to invoke pathos. Nor can we ever pity the gods. By the very fact that they are gods they can never seriously undergo disaster and the outcome of any set of events can never have the significance for them that it does have for human beings.

Hegel has so far spoken primarily of the drama itself. But this does not mean that he believed a play could be divorced from the audience that observes it and the actors that enact it. A play, Hegel insisted, is like a painting in that it does not exist until it becomes incorporated in a meaningful way into some human experience. Of course, the dramatic poet may despise his public as Tieck and Schlegel did. But in that case "he obviously fails to secure the very object for which dramatic writing exists."[96] Hegel felt it was an essential part of the definition of the dramatic composition that "it should possess the vitality able to command a favourable popular reception."[97] To obtain this vitality the artist should submit to several important conditions.

First of all, the poet should consider the audience he wishes to please, and then he should choose those conflicts and situations which would be most apt to please such an audience. If he wishes to reach as much of the public as possible, then his drama should deal either with those perennial problems that cause conflict or with the problems that have arisen in his age and time. It is easier to write about contemporary issues, but the artist should recognize that plays about a contemporary subject matter are most apt to lose their original appeal. Thus, Calderón's works are too parochial and too narrow to have any long-lasting appeal. On the other hand, because of "a profounder psychological penetration and a greater breadth of particular characterization,"[98] Shakespeare and the ancients have succeeded in appealing to men's most fundamental emotions.

A second step that the author can take in his endeavor to obtain a popular reception is to create unique and unforgettable characters. The individual personalities should be presented in such a way that they become memorable as real and vital human beings. The writer ought to be on the constant search for those curious traits that can make a person memorable. A certain kind of smile, or gesture, or manner of speech can create an image that will exactly fit the role the writer seeks to present. This kind of characterization was successfully accomplished by Sophocles, Shakespeare, and Goethe. The French writers, however, have generally "been rather content to excogitate characters that are little more than the formal impersonations of general types and passions, than to have aimed at giving us true and living persons."[99]

However, good characterization can never take the place of action. Goethe's Tasso displays excellent characterization, but its lack of dramatic action makes it fail as a play. In the final analysis action is the one element that every play must possess if it is to be called a play. There must be actual physical movement and change that lead from an initial to a final activity. The action cannot be an intellectual dialogue because the significance of drama as an art form is that it can show us pictures of human action at its most crucial moments. Both words and physical motion are equally important in giving us the developing picture imagined by the writer. A play that is simply "talky" can only partially realize the potentialities of drama as an art form. In fact, sometimes the action itself is sufficient to create a great play. Thus, particular scenes in Greek tragedies may be boring to us. Some scenes may be modified in accordance with new methods of building stages and settings. But the nature of the action itself is such that it can be of perennial interest. Goethe's revision of the barbaric cruelty of the human sacrifice in *Iphigenia* did not mar the greatness of the play. The basic appeal of the action still remained the same.

Hegel was quite explicit about the relation of the drama to the stage. The playwright should always consider his play in terms of the stage and the setting in which it will be enacted. In fact, Hegel opposed the publication and free circulation of a play. "No dramatic work ought to be printed, but rather, as no doubt with the ancients, it should belong to the stage repertory in manuscript form, and only receive quite an insignificant circulation."[100] Any mere recitation of a drama is a detriment to appreciation. "For when we listen to an action we desire to see the acting persons, their demeanour and surroundings; the eye craves for a completed vision, and finds instead before it merely a reciter, who sits or stands peacefully in a private house with company."[101]

For this reason full appreciation of a play is dependent upon the actors who are selected for the roles. Through the ages the importance of the actors has consistently grown. For the Greeks the actor was primarily an instrument for translating into reality the kind of personage depicted by the author. For them the actor was "the instrument upon which the author plays, an artist's brush which absorbs all colours and returns the same unchanged."[102] But in the contemporary drama the actor is given a much greater opportunity for interpretation. Since masks are no longer used, facial expressions are often left to the actor himself. Similarly, the actor can now make a much freer use of gestures. The reason for this is that modern tragedy, more than ancient tragedy, stresses individuality and uniqueness. The characters of Shakespeare, for example, are much more particularized and individualistic than those in the Greek tragedies. As a result, actors have become such significant figures that they can often demand that a poet write dramas expressly for them. Nor is this an unreasonable demand, according to Hegel. Actors should "receive all the honours of an artistic profession. . . . The profession demands conspicuous talent, intelligence, perseverance, energy, practice, knowledge, and, indeed, its highest attainment is impossible without the rare qualities of genius."[103]

According to Hegel, the freedom given to the actor is a characteristic peculiar to the modern age, and leads to a great concern with the psychological makeup of the characters in the play. The actor's personality is now counted as an intrinsic element in the construction of the play. Thus, scenes that highlight the actor himself are brought in to complement the action. This new emphasis on the psychological can be seen when we compare Aeschylus' *Choephorae* and Sophocles' *Electra* to Shakespeare's *Hamlet*. In all these dramas, the king is murdered and the wife has married the murderer. In the Greek plays the real collision turns on the fact that the son, in giving vent to a rightful sense of vengeance, is himself forced to violate the moral code.[104] But in *Hamlet* the collision is almost overshadowed by the analysis made of Hamlet as a person. The basic collision is an elementary one; the revenging son is required to kill a usurping uncle. But the psychological description is so detailed and so emphasized that the collision is made to depend upon it.

> The real collision, therefore, does not turn on the fact that the son, in giving effect to a rightful sense of vengeance, is himself forced to violate morality, but rather on the particular personality, the inner life of Hamlet, whose noble soul is not steeled to this kind of energetic activity, but, while full of contempt for the world and life, what between making up his mind and attempting to carry into effect or preparing to carry into effect its resolves, is bandied from pillar to post, and finally through his own procrastination and the external course of events meets his own doom.[105]

The creation of such introspective and brooding figures as Hamlet and Macbeth is, of course, the work of genius. Shakespeare soars "at an almost unapproachable height"[106] above his contemporaries as well as later writers. In Shakespeare there is the perfect combination of individuality and abstraction. No one, not even Goethe or Schiller, can rival Shakespeare "in the ideal force and exaltation of passion."[107]

Near the conclusion of the *Philosophy of Fine Art,* Hegel briefly considered comedy as an art form. He noted that comedy also requires collision of some sort, but the collision is usually trivial and semi-serious. As a result, the resolution does not provide the emotional impact of tragedy. Comedy depends more upon showing the irrational element of man. Whereas tragedy challenges men to attain greater insights into their own being, comedy accepts man as he is. It emphasizes man's blunders and displays his foolish aspects. But it does it in such a way that no basic threat to or probing of a fundamental belief occurs. For this reason comedy is a kind of escapism used by the lower classes to avoid serious consideration of important problems. Aristophanes' work undoubtedly contained many profound insights, but it was also "one of the greatest symptoms of the degeneracy of Greece."[108]

Finally, Hegel insists that his strong feelings about the significance of tragedy and the lack of significance of comedy do not commit him to the view that tragedy must not contain happy endings. Destiny, Hegel declared, affords both happy and unhappy endings, and therefore it is foolish to think that a tragedy must have one or the other. Personally, Hegel declared, "I prefer a happy conclusion."[109] But, of course, it would be absurd to supply a happy ending to a set of events that make such a conclusion highly improbable. If a man is characterized as a villain throughout a play, we certainly do not expect him to be converted merely for the sake of a happy ending.

IX. CONCLUSION
AND CRITICISM

THROUGHOUT the chapters on the arts I have deliberately avoided critical comments in order to provide a clear exposition wherever possible of some of the specific points that Hegel expressed about the arts. But in this final chapter I should like to evaluate Hegel's aesthetic views to determine whether they have more than historical interest. If the metaphysics of Hegel must be regarded as an essential element of his aesthetics, then contemporary aestheticians can raise serious and damaging objections. However, I will argue that Hegel's metaphysics is not a crucial element in his aesthetics, so that a rejection of the metaphysics does not entail a rejection of the aesthetics. Just as we can read and appreciate Aristotle's *Poetics* even if we reject his ontology, and just as we can obtain some remarkable insights into art by studying John Dewey's *Art as Experience* without being committed to pragmatism or even empiricism, I think we can do the same with Hegel's lectures on aesthetics.

However, before I evaluate his aesthetic theory I should like to note some of the criticisms of his metaphysical position. Hegel assumes that art necessarily evolves through the various phases which he has examined. The cause for this evolution is a force, an all-inclusive essence, which directs the development of art history. But Hegel does not take into account the possibility that art may change for reasons other than the metaphysical one he expounds. Hegel assumes that the artist must be a child of the philosophical and theological climate of his age, and that therefore all artistic endeavors must necessarily reflect the results of such metaphysical speculation. But Hegel overlooks the fact that some great art has little if any connection with either philosophy or theology. The fine works of Adrian Brouwer and Gustave Courbet, to mention but two examples, are clearly lacking in any philosophic interest. Similarly, as Harold Osborne points out, it is generally acknowledged that some lyrical poems by Herrick and Drayton are better than Cowper's *The Task,* but "however you define 'wisdom,' there is more of it in the latter than the former."[1] Art, therefore, does not have a necessary connection with philosophical or theological ideas, although Hegel might still have argued that the inclusion of such ideas gives the art work a higher probability of success.

The alternative theory that Hegel might have considered is that art evolves because of various social pressures. Hauser has argued that changes in art are not due to a driving force in human consciousness which must be made explicit.[2] On the contrary, the direction art takes is determined by the kind of social, political, and economic structure in which the artist is placed. In the Middle Ages the artist found it profitable to employ religious themes in his work. But with the advent of the interest in science and individualism these themes were replaced by an emphasis on realism. The artist was not motivated by any desire to depict the Idea, but rather to depict scenes and motifs which would yield aesthetic satisfaction to the dominant social group.

Nor is Hauser's theory the only alternative to the Hegelian metaphysical scheme. Aestheticians of the formalist school— for example, Fry, Bell, and Osborne—have argued that whereas Hegel saw in Renaissance art the beginnings of deterioration, in reality art since the Renaissance, especially in the nineteenth and twentieth centuries, has just begun to realize its primary potentialities. They claim that medieval and Renaissance painting, for example, only vaguely incorporated the real function of art, namely, the presentation of significant or, as Osborne calls it, "configurational" form.[3] Medieval painting was too involved in presenting religious images to undertake a full examination of the nature of artistic form, but the artists of today have finally extricated themselves from subject matters and interests that are alien to the true artistic function. After all, our sciences have become more mathematical. Why should our arts not become more formalized?

Both the economic and the formalistic interpretations of art may seem extreme and may possibly be incorrect. But the fact remains that they are possible alternatives to the Hegelian analysis.

Another criticism against the Hegelian metaphysics of art is that Hegel never extricates himself from the charge that the Idea is no more than a tautological concept. In his theory any and every development in art is a manifestation of the Idea. But if this is true, then the Idea, as an explanatory device, is in the privileged position of being able to justify the occurrence of any and all events. The Idea could explain everything. But an explanation of this sort is clearly not as cogent as Hegel believed it to be.

If a principle can explain everything, then it can be used to explain *a* if *a* occurs, and *not-a* if *not-a* occurs. By "explanation" we mean an inference from the principle, or generalization, to the particular occurrence to be explained. But if a principle can be used to infer either *a* or *not-a,* then every inference is allowable. The Idea, accordingly, can be used to justify whatever evolution of art is conceived. A classic-romantic-symbolic cycle of art would have been as justified by the Idea as a symbolic-classic-romantic cycle. Of course, Hegel might have argued that the existence of the symbolic-classic-romantic cycle is upheld by the facts. But in this case he is simply telling us what he believes *did* occur. He is not using the Idea to assure us that what did occur inevitably *had* to occur. Hegel sought to use the Idea as a guarantee for a particular evolution of art. But actually the Idea guaranteed too much. By being able to justify everything, it could not guarantee the necessity of anything.

When we apply this criticism more specifically to art works, we find that Hegel's metaphysical criterion can not actually help us to distinguish good from bad art. A work of art is good when it incorporates the Idea; it is bad when it does not. But how are we to tell when a work of art does exemplify the Idea or, at least, a manifestation of the Idea? Hegel might have answered that the mark of the Idea in a painting is the inclusion of a religious concept, and, therefore, this mark is a characteristic of the good painting. But, first of all, not all paintings that incorporate religious themes are good works of art. Secondly, it is often very difficult to determine when a painting lacks a religious theme. In a certain sense any abstract painting can be said to have religious content. A set of lines can be taken to signify the infinite. A black spot on a huge white background can be a symbol of evil in a world of good. If we really wanted to, we could interpret any work of art— good or otherwise—in such a way that the work is seen to portray a manifestation of the Idea. At least this would be possible as long as no appropriate definition of "interpret" is forthcoming. And since Hegel does not supply this definition, the recognition of the Idea in a work of art remains perpetually elusive.

Hegel might have escaped the difficulties mentioned by simply declaring that his theory could not be used to evaluate art products since art products no longer really existed. On one analysis, as Croce and others have noted, Hegel seems to be ringing the funeral knell for art. Artistic creation has run its cycle. Therefore, all future art is either mere imitation or an exercise in manual dexterity. However, as I have indicated, I do not think this is the only way in which Hegel can be read. Hegel may not have considered art to be as significant to human beings as religion and philosophy, but he certainly did not view art as trivial. In the *Philosophy of History*, Hegel specifically states that the flourishing of the fine arts signifies the vitality and inventiveness of a civilization.[4]

There is another criticism that can be levelled against Hegel's metaphysics of art. Hegel believed that the organic changes which take place in living things are also found in society and history. Like living things, social groups and historical events develop in accordance with some hidden force that is seeking to make itself explicit. But there is an essential ambiguity that pervades any theory that clings to the explicit-implicit dichotomy.

Consider, for example, a simple instance in which an oak is sometimes regarded as the explicit expression of all that is implicit in the acorn. What function do the terms "implicit" and "explicit" serve here? As Hume long ago pointed out, we can never know what is "implicit" in the acorn until the result finally appears. And once it has appeared, we can not know that it was really implicit until a similar result has occurred again and again. Otherwise, the result could be a coincidence or a freakish accident. But the fact that an event repeatedly occurs is not sufficient evidence that it had to occur or that *its* occurrence, rather than any other, was part of an implicit design in nature. Under other conditions an acorn might grow into something else, and if this new change continued for any length of time, we would then come to view the sudden appearance of an oak as a freak of nature. In short, all that we mean when we say an event, *B*, is implicit in some other event, *A*, is that *B* has usually appeared whenever we have found *A*. We do not mean that there is something inherent in the structure of things which necessitates the occurrence of *B*. The term "implicit," therefore, if it is to designate anything in experience, can do so only if it is defined so as to refer to the fact that some phenomena continually occur. But such a definition no longer carries with it the connotation of necessity.

This criticism of the implicit-explicit dichotomy is applicable to all phases of Hegel's metaphysics. We believe an oak will occur because of the unfailing appearances of oaks in the past. But since there is only one history and one art evolution, we are unable to say that art will develop in the way that it does because it has done so in numerous previous cycles. On a Spenglerian or Toynbeean analysis this kind of argument might be possible, but it is not possible on an Hegelian analysis. To Hegel, *all* of history and *all* of art are to be viewed as one complete cycle. But he is in the same dilemma as the man who would believe that the acorn must become an oak because he had observed one example of this phenomenon.

It might be argued that Hegel was well-acquainted with art history, that as a philosopher living in the early part of the nineteenth century he was able to study the art that had developed through the centuries and thus abstract the laws of dialectic. The answer to this argument, however, would be the same as that given to the man who, having observed one instance in which one phenomenon follows another, tries to maintain that this conjunction is necessary. It should be obvious that the one instance could have been a coincidence or a freak accident. There is no guarantee of its necessity. Similarly, Hegel may have been right in describing what occurred in art history. He may even have discovered some principle which could order all art history. But he was wrong in attributing to this principle an a priori structure.

A more damaging criticism of Hegel's metaphysics is that it leads him to be careless of or oblivious to some warranted artistic judgments that are not very amenable to the dialectic approach. Thus, to mention only a few examples, Hegel criticizes Giotto as one in whom religious fervor is much less apparent than in earlier painters.[5] Such deterioration, according to Hegel, is a necessary outcome of the inevitable march of the dialectic. But what Hegel ignores is the fact that many of the great paintings by Giotto have been judged to contain a much deeper religious fervor and sincerity than appear in the work of earlier painters. It can be legitimately argued that Giotto's "Madonna and Child Enthroned" has much more religious poignancy and significance than the similar work painted by Cimabue. Similarly, Giotto's "Raising of Lazarus" in the Arena Chapel at Padua is incomparably more religious in theme and mood than a similar work that appears in the Gospels of Otto III of about the year 1000. The dialectic process may have required a steady dissolution of religious art from the early to the late Middle Ages. But Hegel nowhere tells us how we are to deal with the many obvious exceptions.

The tendency to generalize without carefully considering possible exceptions is also evident in Hegel's praise for the Van Eyck brothers. Their works, he claims, have an unsurpassed grace and unity. But the Van Eyck brothers have been consistently criticized for at least one work, "The Adoration of the Lamb," which is said to lack perspective and which includes such an abundance of detail that the unity of the work is destroyed. Also, to Hegel, Correggio is the artist par excellence, one of the greatest of the religious painters. But we have only to note some of the erotic and evil-smiling angels in the "Madonna with St. Jerome" to feel that Correggio is not always the pure painter that Hegel believed him to be.

Similar important exceptions to Hegel's generalizations are found in all the arts. Hegel argues that the standing position is the most suitable for sculpture.[6] But is this meant to deny the excellence of the sitting figures of "Theseus" and of "The Three Fates" found in the last pediment of the Parthenon? Hegel criticizes Egyptian art for being too unnaturalistic, because the details that produce personality and individuality are lacking. But what he overlooks is the fact that Egyptian sculptors *were* naturalistic when it suited their purposes. Naturalistic sculpture portraying action and individual personality marked the reign of Akhenaton between 1375–1358 B.C. In one existent relief, Akhenaton and the lovely Nefertite, are found depicted in extraordinarily naturalistic poses. Both figures are presented in casual manner: the king with crossed legs, resting on a staff, and Nefertite extending flowers to him. Similarly, the animals and fishes on the relief in the Tomb of Ti are far from stiff and unnatural. The head of the Saitic Dignitary that is now in the Museum of Fine Arts in Boston is individualistic to the point of containing a wart under the left eye.

Such exceptions readily come to mind when the Hegelian metaphysical generalizations are closely scrutinized. Few art critics today would be pleased by Hegel's generalizations about art and art history. What then is the value of Hegel's aesthetics for us today?

I think that several important values attach to the Hegelian aesthetic. First of all, an important attempt is made to define experience in such a way that aesthetic as well as cognitive judgments can be legitimately asserted. In the contemporary period we are often inclined to define "experience" as a steady flow of things containing properties and, perhaps, several kinds of basic relationships. Then the assertion is made that a language, or a series of words, is meaningful if and only if these words either refer to the objects, properties, or relationships that are said to define experience or else they are what are called syncategorematic terms, that is, terms that are simply part of the syntactical framework of the language. When a term is encountered which does not belong to one or the other of these two groups, we reject it as meaningless, confused, or subjective. Thus, we have been able to avoid real concern with such words as "good," "bad," "right," "wrong," "ugly," and "beautiful" on the ground that such words are not members of one or the other of the two appropriate categories. But what Hegel has argued is that experience is by no means the simple phenomenon we often take it to be. There are "situations" in experience. Things are sometimes presented to us in the form of purpose and order. Just as we often organize material entities in such a way that a particular purposeful product is created—for example, an automobile—so also we often observe activities out of which a particularly significant action presents itself. We describe this action in numerous ways. We can call it "heroic" or "dramatic" or "pathetic." But however we may describe it, we acknowledge that some actions have a greater significance to us and, perhaps, to mankind than other actions. If we admit this, then we should also agree that there ought to be some way of describing these actions and of inquiring into the characteristics that give them value. Even if we reject Hegel's notion of the Idea, he may still be right in demanding that our language and our inquiries take into account certain situations and events in experience.

Clearly, if Hegel is right—if there is more to experience than things, properties, and certain fundamental relationships—the possibility presents itself of having a genuine subject matter to which art products can refer. It may well be that some occurrences can only be described by a painting or a poem. We are often told that the famous enigmatic face of the Mona Lisa could not be verbally described. Mere reference to a smile or to some other obvious facial expression cannot be sufficient to indicate the subtle shades of meaning that have been blended together. Only the painting could give us that ineffable quality of personality which the "Mona Lisa" reveals to us. Similarly, it may well be that only art can be used to communicate to others the emotions aroused by unusual happenings. We should note how close we come to using the storyteller's form of art when we are recounting something which we consider to be very important. Our words become punctuated by emphases and pauses which mark the initial change of ordinary language into an artistic form. If Hegel's analysis is really correct, it could be a possible answer to the positivistic contention that art has nothing to which it can refer.

Another important aspect of Hegel's views on art is his concern with a number of problems that have been slighted by most contemporary aestheticians. Consider his endeavor to analyze the kind of facial expression that can best convey a sense of holiness or saintliness. Perhaps we no longer worry about such matters, but any painter who deals with the human figure must finally ask himself what the relationship is between a given facial design or a given word and the mood or attitude that is to be felt by an observer. Nor is it strictly a matter of dealing with human figures. The numerous sketches that Picasso drew prior to the final production of "Guernica" testify to the fact that the artist eliminates certain expressions and adds others. Similarly, when John Milton substituted words in his *Comus* for other words, he clearly used some criterion which convinced him that one particular word combination would be more effective than another. Yet little attempt has been made to understand why an artist decides that *this* brush-stroke will be more effective than *that* one, why one word can be more effective than another.

These questions do not refer to the psychology of the artist. They concern the possible discovery of some principle or set of principles whose usage results in good rather than bad art. Hegel is clearly involved in examining these very basic questions. One cannot read his lectures on aesthetics without being fascinated by the almost endless series of problems in art with which Hegel was concerned. Why were the pyramids designed as they were? What makes one curved line more effective than another? Why do human beings respond to rhythms? In a real sense Hegel was an aesthetician for artists, not for other aestheticians. His questions are often so fundamental to the understanding of particular art works that he appears to be one of the most empirical of empiricists. He may be at fault for ignoring many works of art, but in his specific analyses he cannot be accused of ignoring the significant questions.

Thus. even though we have been highly critical of many of Hegel's comments on the specific arts, we should not therefore ignore the significance of his many valuable insights. The student of Greek literature will find in Hegel's work a complete survey of all the theoretical problems that arise in connection with Greek epic and drama. For example, Hegel's analysis of the Greek hero is extremely penetrating and incisive. His conception of the hero as a symbol of the progressive advance of civilization through the development of a higher code of morality deserves close scrutiny. Moreover, while aesthetic inquiry has not particularly concerned itself with the problem of defining the nature of collision and conflict, it is to Hegel's credit that he long ago recognized the importance of these two concepts and attempted, in detailed discussion, to analyze the nature of the unique ethical struggle that permeates heroic action in Greek tragedy.

Hegel's views on architecture are also often seminal and provocative, particularly his discussion of the influence of aesthetic, religious, and scientific ideas on the various forms of architecture. When Hegel elaborately tries to prove that art is a resultant product of the religious and philosophical conceptions that prevail at any given time, he emphasizes a point that is frequently overlooked today: that the values of a civilization are reflected in the styles and ornamentations of its dwellings. Furthermore, although we have criticized Hegel's generalizations about painting and sculpture, we have only praise for the vital portions of his analyses of these arts. His attempt to define the relationship between a physical characteristic and an emotion should be of great interest to contemporary aestheticians. They also consider the connection between a feeling and its expression in a physical medium to be an important relation which needs explication. Nor are Hegel's views on color without merit. His belief that there exists a logical system of colors analogous to a logical system of words and numbers should certainly be challenging to those who, like the cubists, foresee the eventual mathematicising of the different arts.

Even in the area in which he admitted he was weakest—music—Hegel provides us with thought-provoking observations. His theory that our fascination with music is due to the stimulation by sound of certain implicit forms of consciousness reflects a Kantian influence. But it also signifies a major effort to give music a referent that is exempt from the imagery and feelings that have traditionally been mistakenly assumed to be responsible for musical reaction.

Also, it is important to recognize that Hegel was constantly involved in the question of the relation of art to men. He believed that art fulfills a very necessary need in human beings. It gives them a mental conception of value incorporated into action. Scientific terminology is abstract and omits reference either to everyday experience or to values. But art fulfills both requirements. By its appeal to the emotions and the imagination it shows us what we ought to try to become and what we ought to consider valuable.

In conclusion, we should note the extensiveness of Hegel's knowledge of the arts. Who has ever brought so much erudition to the study of aesthetics! The contemporary aesthetician thinks himself fortunate if he brings to his inquiries knowledge of a particular art. But Hegel had accumulated a fantastic amount of information about all the arts. In this book I have only been able to refer to a very small number of the numerous works which Hegel uses to support his generalizations. Thus, while Hegel's metaphysics can be sharply criticized, his aesthetics cannot be dismissed lightly. Undoubtedly his inquiry into the nature of action and his attempt to reassess experience can be of genuine importance to the contemporary student of aesthetics.

NOTES

Chapter I. THE IDEA

1. Hegel's *Phenomenology of Mind* should also be mentioned,
although it does not contain the close-knit inquiry into the nature of
thought that appears in the logical treatises, especially the *Science
of Logic.*

2. J. M. E. McTaggart pointed out that Kant was not really even
permitted to say that the thing-in-itself is. This is a judgment, "and
a judgment involves categories, and we are thus forced to surrender
the idea that we can be aware of the existence of anything which is
not subject to the laws governing experience" (*Studies in the Hegelian Dialectic* [2d ed.; Cambridge: Cambridge University Press, 1922],
p. 27). Nor does Paton answer this objection to Kant by maintaining

that the noumena are the "condition" of the appearance of phe. nomena. How can the noumena be the condition of the appearance of phenomena without implying that there is a causal connection between noumena and phenomena? See H. J. Paton, *Kant's Metaphysic of Experience* (London: George Allen and Unwin, 1936), I, 62.

3. *Critique of Pure Reason,* translated by F. Max Muller (2d ed., rev.; New York: Macmillan Co., 1934), pp. 66 ff.

4. The nature of these derivations was not clearly presented by Kant, and in most instances the derivations were arbitrary. See N. K. Smith, *A Commentary on Kant's Critique of Pure Reason* (London: Macmillan Co., 1918), pp. 194 ff.

5. *SW,* Lasson, IV, 253. See also *Science of Logic,* translated by Johnston and Struthers (New York: Macmillan Co., 1929), II, 247.

6. *SW,* Lasson, V, 69; *Encyclopedical Logic,* translated by Wallace (2d ed., rev.; Oxford: Clarendon Press, 1892), p. 88.

7. Generally, Kant's views seemed to invalidate the possibility of any such deduction. If the categories were derived from some general principle, then, to avoid a *petitio principii,* we would have the curious paradox of accepting a principle as cognitive, although it had not been derived from a categorized and spatio-temporalized subject matter. But the *Critique of Pure Reason* had explicitly stated that legitimate cognitive doctrines could be obtained only from an experiential context. Of course, Kant had distinguished between the principles of the understanding and those of reason. The principles of reason, however, were regulative and not cognitive principles. The task of reason was simply to point out the contradictions that resulted when the categories of the understanding were used in the unknowable realm of the noumena. Kant, therefore, had not stipulated principles of reason from which the categories could be deduced. Nor, for that matter, was Kant's conception of the unity of apperception able to serve as the primary principle. Kant had insisted upon the unity which characterized the categories, but this unification had simply been posited. Kant had not explained the nature of this unification, whether it entailed the deduction of the categories from the Ego or some higher principle. And even if such a deduction were implicit in Kant's work, it contained no attempt to show precisely how this deduction was to be made.

8. Hegel insisted that it was the very essence of life to be involved in contradiction. But the contradiction did not remain unresolved. "Das Lebendige aber hat die Kraft, den Widerspruch zu ertragen und ihn immer aufzulösen" (*SW,* Lasson, Xa, 172). See also McTaggart's interesting comments in his *Studies in the Hegelian Dialectic,* pp.

131-32.

9. *Encyclopedical Logic*, p. 120.

10. *SW*, Lasson, III, 54; *Science of Logic*, I, 82.

11. *Studies in the Hegelian Dialectic*, p. 20.

12. *SW*, Lasson, V, 134; *Encyclopedical Logic*, p. 229. For this reason Mure is not correct when he states that for Hegel "all judgment is both predicative and existential" (*Introduction to Hegel* [Oxford: Clarendon Press, 1940], pp. 143-44). First of all, existence as a category occurs only after experience has undergone a more extensive development. Secondly, the existential judgment is an outcome of mediated experience, i.e., of experience which is not mere primitive immediacy. According to Hegel, existence can be attributed to a state of affairs only after implicit causal and logical relationships have been made explicit. This is what Hegel means when he states, "For das Sein, welches vermittelt ist, werden wir den Ausdruck: Existenz, aufbehalten" (*SW*, Lasson, III, 78; *Science of Logic*, I, 105), and elsewhere that "die Existenz ist dies aus dem Aufheben der durch Grund und Bedingung beziehenden Vermittlung hervor gegangene Unmittekbarkeit, dies im Hervorgehen eben dies Hervor gehen selbst aufhebt" (*SW*, Lasson, IV, 102; *Science of Logic*, III, 109).

13. *Encyclopedical Logic*, p. 161.

14. *Ibid.*, p. 159.

15. *SW*, Lasson, III, 66-67; *Science of Logic*, I, 94.

16. *SW*, Lasson, III, 77-78; *Science of Logic*, I, 104.

17. *SW*, Lasson, III, 70 ff.; *Science of Logic*, I, 97 ff.

18. For some fundamental criticisms made by neo-Hegelians see G. R. G. Mure, *A Study of Hegel's Logic* (Oxford: Clarendon Press, 1950), p. 357; J. M. E. McTaggart, *A Commentary on Hegel's Logic* (Cambridge: Cambridge University Press, 1910), p. 5, and *Studies in the Hegelian Dialectic*, ch. iv; Benedetto Croce, *What is Living and What is Dead of the Philosophy of Hegel*, translated by D. Ainslie (London: Macmillan Co., 1915), pp. 185-91; W. T. Stace, *The Philosophy of Hegel* (New York: Macmillan Co., 1924), p. 315; J. Loewenberg, editor, *Hegel Selections* (New York: Charles Scribner's Sons, 1929), p. xxxviii.

19. Hegel's Idea must not be identified, as it sometimes has been, with a universal characterizing an entire class. Such a universal does not entail for Hegel the varied and concrete content that the Idea does. See *SW*, Lasson, V, 160 and 10a, 159 ff.; *Science of Logic*, II, 222; *Encyclopedical Logic*, p. 295.

20. *Encyclopedical Logic*, pp. 341 ff.

21. *Ibid.*, pp. 358 ff.

22. Technically, the Absolute Idea refers to the concept that can only be attained in philosophic speculation. In his logical treatises Hegel distinguished between the term "Idea" and the more technical term "Absolute Idea." However, in the *Philosophy of Fine Art* Hegel referred indiscriminately to the Idea as well as the Absolute Idea. The distinction is not a crucial one, and we should understand Hegel as referring to the same concept when he uses such terms as Idea, Absolute Idea, God, Notion, Absolute, and Divine Process.

23. It was probably C. S. Peirce's awareness of Hegel's difficulty in deducing a specific existential statement that made him remark that Hegel's metaphysics is a "model of a philosophy that in reality does not exist" (*Collected Papers,* edited by Hartshorne and Weiss [Cambridge, Mass., Harvard University Press, 1935], VI, 204).

Chapter II. THE IDEA IN ART

1. Hegel distinguishes between correct and truthful definitions. It would be correct to say that reference to emotion must be part of the definition of beauty, but it is not the entire truth. See *Encyclopedical Logic,* pp. 305, 352, 354.

2. The artist must have knowledge. Imagination by itself is not sufficient. But this knowledge does not have to be in the technical and precise form that the philosopher gives it. "Aus der Leichfertigkeit der Phantasie geht kein gediegenes Werk hervor. Damit soll jedoch nicht gesagt sein, dass der Künstler das Wahrhaftige aller Dinge, welches wie in der Religion so auch in der Philosophie und Kunst die allgemeine Grundlage ausmacht, in Form philosophischer Gedanken ergreifen müsse" (*SW,* Lasson, Xa, 371; *PFA,* I, 382).

3. *SW,* Lasson, Xa, 245 ff.; *PFA,* I, 236.

4. *PFA,* I, 246.

5. *SW,* Lasson, Xa, 251; *PFA,* I, 241.

6. *SW,* Lasson, Xa, 271; *PFA,* I, 257.

7. *SW,* Lasson, Xa, 275; *PFA,* I, 263.

8. *SW,* Lasson, Xa, 278; *PFA,* I, 266.

9. *SW,* Lasson, Xa, 279; *PFA,* I, 266. It might be noted that in his analysis of experience, John Dewey also refers to the resolution of an experience that has gone through the phases of indeterminate and then determinate situations. See *Logic, the Theory of Inquiry* (New York: Henry Holt and Co., 1938).

10. *SW,* Lasson, Xa, 281; *PFA,* I, 267.

11. *SW,* Lasson, Xa, 286; *PFA,* I, 272. The conflict, however, cannot be strictly psychological. Emphasis on the psychological can be very strong as, for example, in *Hamlet,* but the conflict must also involve genuine physical activity.

12. *Ibid.*

13. *SW*, Lasson, Xa, 296; *PFA*, I, 284. See also note 11 above. The psychological conflict must also be expressed in behavior. Hamlet does not only brood; he also causes external events which evolve inevitably towards their conclusion.

14. See *A Kierkegaard Anthology*, edited by Robert Bretall (Princeton: Princeton University Press, 1946), pp. 42, 118.

15. *PFA*, I, 292. The collision of these powers cannot be treated adequately in any art except the drama. On this point see also A. C. Bradley, "Hegel's Theory of Tragedy," *Oxford Lectures on Poetry* (2d ed.; London: Macmillan Co., 1909), pp. 71 ff.

16. *SW*, Lasson, Xa, 301; *PFA*, I, 291.

17. *PFA*, I, 290.

18. See Chapter VIII.

19. *SW*, Lasson, Xa, 323; *PFA*, I, 317.

20. For Sophocles, Hegel declared, the conflict between Polyneices and Etpocles is not simply a fight for the throne. Sophocles "is at pains to shift the quarrel of the brothers on to still more fateful circumstances" (*SW*, Lasson, Xa, 288; *PFA*, I, 277). The conflict is taken to symbolize a more profound collision involving basic moral values.

Chapter III. THE SYMBOLIC STAGE OF ART: ARCHITECTURE

1. *SW*, Glockner, XIII, 244; *PFA*, III, 5. However, the dialectic of art must not be regarded as strictly evolutionary. Not in all cases does later art represent better art. George Boas has maintained that for Hegel the earlier stages of art "were primitive not merely in the sense of being first, but in the sense of being rudimentary, inchoate elements of what was to come" (*Wingless Pegasus* [Baltimore: Johns Hopkins Press, 1950], pp. 140-41). However, in a given cycle of art— as, for example, in the organic development of symbolism—the final stage of symbolism is not more advanced than previous ones. It is a deterioration. See *SW*, Glockner, XII, 505; *PFA*, II, 109.

2. *SW*, Glockner, XIII, 245; *PFA*, III, 6.

3. *SW*, Glockner, XIII, 246; *PFA*, III, 6.

4. *SW*, Glockner, XIII, 247; *PFA*, III, 8. Hegel believed that most philosophers dealt primarily with universals in the sense of abstractions from particulars. For example, after seeing many instances of a red patch the concept "red" is abstracted. Hegel, however, sought to understand the universal which combined discrete entities into a unified whole. As Croce stated: "Why should not the philosophic

universal, like the aesthetic expression, be both at once difference and unity, discord and concord, discrete and continuous, permanent and ever-changing?" (*What is Living and What is Dead of the Philosophy of Hegel* [London: Macmillan Co., 1915], p. 19). Kant also felt the need to analyze this different kind of universal. There is a difference between passively unifying particulars into the concept "red patch" and "combining data of these and a multitude of other sorts into the kind of imaginative composition which we would call, say, a centaur, a limerick, or a piece of music" (S. Körner, *Kant* [Baltimore: Penguin Books, Inc., 1955], p. 47).

5. *SW*, Glockner, XIII, 249; *PFA*, III, 10.

6. *SW*, Glockner, XIII, 248; *PFA*, III, 9. However, a recent art historian has commented: "*Primitive art* used to carry a strong connotation that the artist was unenlightened and knew no better, but that the speaker did. Serious and sympathetic study of earlier civilizations, or those isolated from European influence, has inclined our more recent opinion to caution. Mature reflection very often suggests that the so-called 'primitive' peoples were in fact extremely sophisticated, and that their apparent crudity often denotes profound wisdom expressed with devastating directness" (John Ives Sewall, *A History of Western Art* [New York: Henry Holt and Co., 1953], p. 42).

7. *SW*, Glockner, XII, 422; *PFA*, II, 23.

8. *SW*, Glockner, XII, 423; *PFA*, II, 24. This initial recognition is an important step in the development of art. The cleavage between the immediate existence and its significance has now become apparent, and this breach stimulates the search for unity. "Mit diesem Versuche entsteht das eigentliche Bedürfniss der Kunst" (*SW*, Glockner, XII, 445; *PFA*, II, 47).

9. *SW*, Glockner, XII, 423; *PFA*, II, 24.

10. *Ibid.*

11. "Symbol überhaupt ist eine für die Anschauung unmittelbar vorhandene oder gegebene äusserliche Existenz, welche jedoch nicht so, wie sie unmittelbar vorliegt, ihrer selbst wegen genommen, sondern in einem weiteren und allgemeineren Sinne verstanden werden soll" (*SW*, Glockner, XII, 408; *PFA*, II, 8). The fact that the relationship between symbol and significance is ambiguous is for Hegel an asset for inquiry, since completely fixed relationships would make further advances in knowledge impossible. See the similar observation made by H. H. Price, *Thinking and Experience* (Cambridge, Mass.: Harvard University Press, 1953), p. 95.

12. *SW*, Glockner, XII, 433 ff.; *PFA*, II, 35 ff.

13. *SW*, Glockner, XII, 436; *PFA*, II, 39.

14. *PFA*, II, 45.

15. *SW*, Glockner, XII, 451; *PFA*, II, 53.

16. *SW*, Glockner, XII, 466; *PFA*, II, 68-69.

17. *SW*, Glockner, XIII, 289; *PFA*, III, 49.

18. *SW*, Glockner, XIII, 334; *PFA*, III, 91.

19. *SW*, Glockner, XIII, 346-47; *PFA*, III, 103.

20. *SW*, Glockner, XII, 489-90; *PFA*, II, 93.

21. *SW*, Glockner, XII, 510; *PFA*, II, 114-15. In this kind of writing Hegel also included the Parable, the Proverb, the Apologue, the Metamorphosis, the Metaphor, the Image, and the Simile.

22. "Wenn jedoch nichts der Begriff der Sache selbst, sondern nur die Willkür es ist, die den Inhalt und die Kunstgestalt zueinander-bringt, so sind Beide auch als einander vollständig äusserlich zu setzen, so dass ihr Zusammenkommen ein beziehungsloses Aneinanderfügen und blosses Aufschmücken der einen Seite durch die andere wird" (*SW*, Glockner, XII, 557; *PFA*, II, 162).

Chapter IV. THE CLASSICAL STAGE OF ART: SCULPTURE

1. *SW*, Glockner, XIII, 12; *PFA*, II, 178.

2. *SW*, Glockner, XIII, 11, *PFA*, II, 177. Other animal forms exhibit faint suggestions of spiritual behavior, but only in man is such behavior explicitly revealed.

3. "Der menschliche Ausdruck in Gesicht, Auge, Stellung, Geberde ist zwar materiell, und darin nicht das, was der Geist ist, aber innerhalb dieser Körperlichkeit selbst ist das menschliche Aeussere nicht nur lebendig und natürlich wie das Their, sondern die Leiblichkeit, welche in sich den Geist wiederspiegelt" (*SW*, Glockner, XIII, 11; *PFA*, II, 177).

4. *SW*, Glockner, XIII, 12; *PFA*, II, 178.

5. *Ibid.*

6. *SW*, Glockner, XIII, 14-15; *PFA*, II, 180.

7. *SW*, Glockner, XIII, 18; *PFA*, II, 184.

8. *Ibid.*

9. *SW*, Glockner, XIII, 27; *PFA*, II, 192. Animism permeated the early stages of Judaism. See John B. Noss, *Man's Religions* (New York: Macmillan Co., 1949), pp. 476 ff.

10. *SW*, Glockner, XIII, 31; *PFA*, II, 195.

11. *SW*, Glockner, XIII, 35; *PFA*, II, 199.

12. *SW*, Glockner, XIII, 48; *PFA*, II, 212.

13. *SW*, Glockner, XIII, 64; *PFA*, II, 227. Gradually the Titans "are supplanted by shapes, which do but darkly recall those earlier titans, and which are no longer things of nature, but clear ethical

spirits of self-conscious nations." (*Phenomenology of Mind*, translated by J. B. Baillie [2d ed., rev.; London: George Allen & Unwin, 1931), pp. 714-15).

14. *Ibid.*

15. *SW*, Glockner, XIII, 69; *PFA*, II, 231.

16. Their subject matter "ist dem menschlichen Geist und Dasehn entnommen, und dadurch das Eigene der menschlichen Brust, ein Gehalt, mit welchem der Mensch frei als mit sich selber zusammengehn kann, indem, was er hervorbringt, das schönste Erzeugniss seiner selbst ist" (*SW*, Glockner, XIII, 70; *PFA*, II, 232-33).

17. "So geht das Geschäft der Dichter auch darauf, die Gegenwart und Wirksamkeit der Götter in dieser Bezüglichkeit auf menschliche Dinge zu erkennen, das Besondere der Naturereignisse, der menschlichen Thaten und Schicksale, worein die göttlichen Mächte verflochten erscheinen, zu deuten, und dadurch das Geschäft des Priesters, des Mantis, zu theilen" (*SW*, Glockner, XIII, 71; *PFA*, II, 233-34).

18. *Ibid.*

19. *SW*, Glockner, XIII, 74; *PFA*, II, 236.

20. *SW*, Glockner, XIII, 82-83; *PFA*, II, 244-45.

21. The kind of impression that the Greek gods give, Hegel maintained, is similar to the impression received when one observes a portrait or bust of Goethe. Hegel was highly impressed by Goethe as a man and as a thinker. See *SW*, Glockner, XIII, 76-77; *PFA*, II, 238-39.

22. *SW*, Glockner, XIII, 92; *PFA*, II, 253-54.

23. *SW*, Glockner, XIII, 354-55; *PFA*, III, 111.

24. *SW*, Glockner, XIII, 355; *PFA*, III, 111.

25. *SW*, Glockner, XIII, 435; *PFA*, III, 188.

26. "Ausser dem Denken und dessen philosophischer systematischer Thätigkeit führt der Geist jedoch noch ein volles Leben der Empfindung, Neigung, Vorstellung, Phantasie u.s.f., das in näherem oder weiterem Zusammenhange mit seinem Dasehn als Seele und Leiblichkeit steht, und daher auch am menschlichen Körper eine Realität hat. In dieser ihm selber angehörigen Realität macht sich der Geist gleichfalls lebendig, scheint in sie dinein, durchdringt sie, und wird durch sie für Andere offenbar" (*SW*, Glockner, XIII, 371; *PFA*, III, 127-28).

27. *SW*, Glockner, XIII, 359; *PFA*, III, 115.

28. *SW*, Glockner, XIII, 360; *PFA*, III, 116.

29. *SW*, Glockner, XIII, 362; *PFA*, III, 118.

30. *SW*, Glockner, XIII, 367; *PFA*, III, 123.

31. *SW*, Glockner, XIII, 368; *PFA*, III, 124.

32. *SW*, Glockner, XIII, 368-69; *PFA*, III, 124-25.

33. *SW*, Glockner, XIII, 374; *PFA*, III, 130-31.

34. *SW*, Glockner, XIII, 375; *PFA*, III, 131.

35. *SW*, Glockner, XIII, 453; *PFA*, III, 204.

36. Winckelmann's work appeared in 1764. Although most contemporary art historians reject much of Winckelmann's criticism and analysis, the influence he has exerted has been enormous. One art historian notes that even though Winckelmann's views are often wrong on details, "his critical estimates, however, have become part of our folklore; the man in the street who never heard of Winckelmann will nevertheless quote him if asked to express an opinion about art. No other art historian has had a comparable influence upon European taste" (John Ives Sewall, *A History of Western Art* [New York: Henry Holt and Co., 1953], p. 7).

37. *SW*, Glockner, XIII, 453; *PFA*, III, 205.

38. *SW*, Glockner, XIII, 454; *PFA*, III, 205.

39. *SW*, Glockner, XIII, 377; *PFA*, III, 133.

40. From 1801-1810 Lord Elgin succeeded in shipping most of the remaining sculpture in the Parthenon to London. The sculpture was finally placed in the British Museum.

41. *SW*, Glockner XIII, 382; *PFA*, III, 139.

42. *SW*, Glockner, XIII, 391; *PFA*, III, 147.

43. *Ibid.* Hegel noted further that the forehead was made wider or narrower in accordance with how dignified and serious the personage was considered to be.

44. *SW*, Glockner, XIII, 398; *PFA*, III, 154.

45. *Ibid.*

46. *SW*, Glockner, XIII, 401; *PFA*, III, 157.

47. *SW*, Glockner, XIII, 402; *PFA*, III, 157.

48. *SW*, Glockner, XIII, 406; *PFA*, III, 161.

49. *SW*, Glockner, XIII, 409; *PFA*, III, 164.

50. *SW*, Glockner, XIII, 431; *PFA*, III, 184.

51. *SW*, Glockner, XIII, 432; *PFA*, III, 185. Hegel uses both the Roman and the Greek names of the gods.

52. *SW*, Glockner, XIII, 424; *PFA*, III, 178.

53. *Ibid.* Female figures are usually treated much more delicately. But in many cases there is no marked distinction between masculine and feminine figures. The more youthful figures of Bacchus and Apollo are often depicted as feminine. In fact, Hercules is sometimes confused with Iole, his sweetheart.

54. *SW*, Glockner, XIII, 432-33, *PFA*, III, 185.

55. *SW*, Glockner, XIII, 78; *PFA*, II, 240.

56. *Ibid.*

57. *Ibid.*
58. *Ibid.*
59. *SW,* Glockner, XIII, 79; *PFA,* II, 241.
60. *SW,* Glockner, XIII, 98; PFA, II, 259.
61. *SW,* Glockner, XIII, 93; *PFA,* II, 254.
62. "Das Wesentlichste, was bei dieser Gruppe in Betracht kommt, ist, dass bei dem hohen Schmerz, der hohen Wahrheit, dem krampfhaften zusammenziehn des Körpers, dem Bäumen aller Muskeln, dennoch der Adel der Schönheit erhalten, und zur Grimasse, Verzerrung und Verrenkung auch nicht in der entferntesten Weise fortgegangen ist" (*SW,* Glockner, XIII, 439; *PFA,* III, 191).
63. *SW,* Glockner, XIII, 98; *PFA,* II, 259.
64. *SW,* Glockner, XIII, 461; *PFA,* III, 212.
65. *SW,* Glockner, XIII, 462; *PFA,* III, 213.
66. *SW,* Glockner, XIII, 463; *PFA,* III, 214.
67. *SW,* Glockner, XIII, 464; *PFA,* III, 215.
68. *SW,* Glockner, XIII, 465; *PFA,* III, 216.

Chapter V. THE ROMANTIC STAGE OF ART

1. *SW,* Glockner, XIII, 119; *PFA,* II, 279.
2. *SW,* Glockner, XIII, 126; *PFA,* II, 287.
3. *SW,* Glockner, XIII, 127; *PFA,* II, 288.
4. *SW,* Glockner, XIII, 104-5; *PFA,* II, 265-66.
5. *SW,* Glockner, XIII, 142; *PFA,* II, 302.
6. "Insofern nun aber in dieser Erscheinung der Accent darauf gelegt ist, dass Gott wesentlich ein einzelnes Subjekt mit Ausschluss Anderer seh, und nicht nur die Einheit göttlicher und menschlicher Subjecktivität im Allgemeinen, sondern dieselbe als dieser Mensch darstelle, so treten hier in der Kunft, des Inhalts selbst wegen, alle Seiten der Zufälligkeit und Partikularität des äussern endlichen Dasehns wieder hervor, von welchen sich die Schönheit auf der Höhe des klassischen Ideals gereinigt hatte" (*SW,* Glockner, XIII, 144-45; *PFA,* II, 304).
7. *SW,* Glockner, XIII, 145; *PFA,* II, 304-5.
8. *SW,* Glockner, XIII, 149; *PFA,* II, 309.
9. *SW,* Glockner, XIII, 150; *PFA,* II, 310.
10. *Ibid.*
11. *SW,* Glockner, XIII, 157; *PFA,* II, 317.
12. *Ibid.*
13. *SW,* Glockner, XIII, 160; *PFA,* II, 320.
14. "So fällt nun auch die negative Haltung des zunächst ausschliesslich religiösen Gemüths gegen das Menschliche als solches hinweg, der Geist breitet sich aus, steht sich um in seiner Gegenwart,

und erweitert sein wirkliches weltliches Herz" (*SW*, Glockner, XIII, 166; *PFA*, II, 326).

15. *SW*, Glockner, XIII, 167; *PFA*, II, 327.

16. *SW*, Glockner, XIII, 172; *PFA*, II, 332.

17. See Nicolas Berdyaev, *Slavery and Freedom* (New York: Charles Scribner's Sons, 1944), Pt. I, Chap. I. For several excellent selections dealing with the existentialist emphasis on personality, see also *Four Existentialist Theologians,* edited by Will Herberg (New York: Doubleday & Co., 1958).

18. *SW*, Glockner, XIII, 174; *PFA*, II, 333.

19. *SW*, Glockner, XIII, 174; *PFA*, II, 334.

20. *SW*, Glockner, XIII, 176; *PFA*, II, 335.

21. *SW*, Glockner, XIII, 173; *PFA*, II, 332.

22. *SW*, Glockner, XIII, 167; *PFA*, II, 327.

23. *SW*, Glockner, XIII, 182; *PFA*, II, 341.

24. *Ibid.*

25. *SW*, Glockner, XIII, 180; *PFA*, II, 339.

26. *Ibid.*

27. *SW*, Glockner, XIII, 180; *PFA*, II, 340.

28. *SW*, Glockner, XIII, 186; *PFA*, II, 345.

29. *SW*, Glockner, XIII, 189; *PFA*, II, 348.

30. *Ibid.*

31. "Da ist nicht von Religiosität und von einem Handeln aus religiöser Versöhnung des Menschen in sich, und vom Sittlichen als solchen die Rede. Wir haben im Gegentheil Individuen vor uns, selbständig nur auf sich selber gestellt, mit besondern Zwecken, die nur die ihrigen sind, aus ihrer Individualität allein sich herschreiben, und welche sie nun mit der unerschütterten Konsequenz der Leidenschaft, ohne Nebenreflexion und Allgemeinheit, nur zur eigenen Selbstbefriedigung durchsetzen" (*SW*, Glockner, XIII, 196-97; *PFA*, II, 356).

32. *SW*, Glockner, XIII, 197; *PFA*, II, 356-57.

33. *SW*, Glockner, XIII, 203; *PFA*, II, 362.

34. *SW*, Glockner, XIII, 204; *PFA*, II, 264.

35. *SW*, Glockner, XIII, 212; *PFA*, II, 372.

36. *Ibid.*

37. *SW*, Glockner, XIII, 214; *PFA*, II, 373.

38. *Ibid.*

39. *SW*, Glockner, XIII, 214; *PFA*, II, 374. However, Hegel admitted that there is a fascinating consistency in Don Quixote's madness. His error lies in seeking to uphold a set of values that have become outmoded by the evolution of more inclusive social theories.

40. *SW*, Glockner, XIII, 230; *PFA*, II, 390.

41. *SW,* Glockner, XIII, 217; *PFA,* II, 376.

42. *SW,* Glockner, XIII, 232; *PFA,* II, 392.

43. "The Aesthetic of Hegel is thus a funeral oration: he passes in review the successive forms of art, shows the progressive steps of internal consumption and lays the whole in its grave, leaving Philosophy to write its epitaph" (Benedetto Croce, *Aesthetic,* translated by D. Ainslie [rev. ed.; London: Macmillan Co., 1922], pp. 302-3).

44. *SW,* Glockner, XIII, 238; *PFA,* II, 398.

45. *SW,* Glockner, XIII, 238; *PFA,* II, 399.

46. *SW,* Glockner, XIII, 240; *PFA,* II, 400.

Chapter VI. THE ROMANTIC STAGE OF ART: PAINTING

1. "Der Punkt der inneren Subjektivität, die Lebendigkeit des Gemüths, die Seele der eigensten Empfindung hat die blicklose Gestalt weder zur Koncentration des Innern zusammengefasst, noch zur geistigen Bewegegung, zur Unterscheidung vom Aeussern und zur innern Unterscheidung aus einander getrieben" (*SW,* Glockner, XIV, 9; *PFA,* III, 223).

2. *SW,* Glockner, XIV, 82; *PFA,* III, 295.

3. *SW,* Glockner, XIV, 35; *PFA,* III, 249. See Schopenhauer's comments in this connection. "A shrieking Laocoön could not be produced in marble, but only a figure with the mouth open vainly endeavoring to shriek; a Laocoön whose voice has stuck in his throat, *vox faucibus haesit.* The essence of shrieking, and consequently its effect upon the onlooker, lies entirely in sound; not in the distortion of the mouth" (*The World as Will and Idea,* translated by R. B. Haldane and J. Kemp [8th ed.; London: Kegan Paul, Trench, Trubner and Co., 1883], I, 294).

4. *SW,* Glockner, XIV, 82; *PFA,* III, 295.

5. *SW,* Glockner, XIV, 10; *PFA,* III, 224.

6. *SW,* Glockner, XIV, 17; *PFA,* III, 231. "It is one thing for the mind to have before it a mere Thing—such as the Host *per se,* a piece of stone or wood, or a wretched daub—quite another thing for it to contemplate a painting, rich in thought and sentiment, or a beautiful work of sculpture, in looking at which, soul holds converse with soul and Spirit with Spirit" (*Philosophy of History,* translated by J. Sibree [New York: Collier and Son, 1902], p. 512).

7. *SW,* Glockner, XIV, 14-15; *PFA,* III, 228.

8. However, Hegel admitted that most of the small number of Greek paintings that have been discovered show an extraordinary excellence. See *SW,* Glockner, XIV, 12-13; *PFA,* III, 226.

9. *SW,* Glockner, XIV, 14; *PFA,* III, 228.

10. *SW*, Glockner, XIV, 13-14; *PFA*, III, 227.

11. *SW*, Glockner, XIV, 103-4; *PFA*, III, 316.

12. Hegel credits most of his comments on Italian art to Carl Friedrich von Rumohr (1785–1843), whose *Italiensche Forschungen* was highly influential. Rumohr, however, was opposed to Hegel's idealistic approach to art. He stressed the importance of craftsmanship and technique. See Katherine E. Gilbert and Helmut Kuhn, *A History of Esthetics* (rev. and enl. ed.; Bloomington, Ind.: Indiana University Press, 1953), p. 544.

13. *SW*, Glockner, XIV, 110; *PFA*, III, 322–23.

14. *SW*, Glockner, XIV, 111; *PFA*, III, 323–24.

15. *SW*, Glockner, XIV, 115; *PFA*, III, 327–28.

16. *SW*, Glockner, XIV, 116; *PFA*, III, 329.

17. *SW*, Glockner, XIV, 38; *PFA*, III, 252.

18. *Ibid.*

19. *SW*, Glockner, XIV, 39; *PFA*, III, 252.

20. *SW*, Glockner, XIV, 42; *PFA*, III, 255.

21. *Ibid.*

22. *SW*, Glockner, XIV, 49; *PFA*, III, 263.

23. *Ibid.*

24. *SW*, Glockner, XIV, 50–51; *PFA*, III, 264. Note also Hegel's entertaining remark that just as people so easily attribute spiritual interest to the glance upward, so also they find it easy to prove that there is a religious foundation to every society by merely quoting a few Biblical texts rather than by presenting real proof. "Es ist leicht, ja zu leicht, einem Bilde dadurch ein höheres Interesse zu geben, dass die Hauptfigur den Blick gen Himmel, ins Jenseitige hinein hebt, wie denn auch heutigen Tags diess leichte Mittel gebraucht wird, Gott, die Religion zur Grundlage des Staats zu machen, oder alles und jedes, statt aus der Vernunft der Wirklichkeit, mit Bibelstellen zu erweisen" (*SW*, Glockner, XIV, 50; *PFA*, III, 264).

25. *SW*, Glockner, XIV, 51; *PFA*, III, 265.

26. *SW*, Glockner, XIV, 32; *PFA*, III, 245.

27. *SW*, Glockner, XIV, 18; *PFA*, III, 232.

28. *SW*, Glockner, XIV, 57–58; *PFA*, III, 271. Hegel is here reiterating the point made by Kant that we can be sure that an experience is aesthetic only once we have ascertained that no practical desire is really involved. See *Critique of Aesthetic Judgment*, translated by J. C. Meredith (London: Oxford at the Clarendon Press, 1911), pp. 48 ff.

29. *SW*, Glockner, XIV, 59; *PFA*, III, 272.

30. *SW*, Glockner, XIV, 97; *PFA*, III, 309-10. Harold Osborne has also remarked: "In the practical conduct of life but a small part of the

mind is devoted to awareness of perceptual situations. . . . It is only in the contemplation of aesthetic objects that the full exercise of a trained perceptive faculty is called forth and stimulated to ever greater keenness. . . . Only works of art can stimulate and offer scope for this heightening of consciousness in awareness" (*Aesthetics and Criticism* [New York: Philosophical Library, 1955], pp. 250-51). However, Hegel would probably have not been at all sympathetic to Osborne's attempt to identify this increased awareness with a sudden recognition of pure form.

31. *SW*, Glockner, XIV, 97; *PFA*, III, 309.

32. *Ibid.*

33. *Ibid.*

34. *SW*, Glockner, XIV, 98; *PFA*, III, 311.

35. *SW*, Glockner, XIV, 99; *PFA*, III, 311.

36. *SW*, Glockner, XIV, 62; *PFA*, III, 275.

37. *SW*, Glockner, XIV, 62; *PFA*, III, 275-76.

38. *SW*, Glockner, XIV, 63; *PFA*, III, 276.

39. *SW*, Glockner, XIV, 66; *PFA*, III, 280. Hegel implied that the artist must use colors in accordance with the mood or attitude he wishes to convey. Thus, if tranquility is to be indicated in the painting, more blue should be used. However, Hegel ignored the fact that the psychological association of color and emotion is changeable. Under some circumstances blue can suggest thunder and war. Furthermore, the artist might obtain more effective results by violating such conventional associations. See L. A. Reid, *Study in Aesthetics* (London: Allen and Unwin Co., 1931), p. 98.

40. *SW*, Glockner, XIV, 68; *PFA*, III, 281.

41. Green is not, of course, a cardinal color. This error may have been due to the fact that Hegel accepted Goethe's false theory of color rather than that of Newton.

42. *SW*, Glockner, XIV, 17; *PFA*, III, 231.

43. Kant believed that one could attribute beauty to a pattern or symmetrical form. But such beauty ought not to be confused with the genuine, or *free*, beauty which attaches to meaningful objects that can be admired for their own sake. See *Critique of Aesthetic Judgment*, translated by J. C. Meredith, pp. 72 ff.

44. *SW*, Glockner, XIV, 124; *PFA*, III, 337.

Chapter VII. THE ROMANTIC STAGE OF ART: MUSIC

1. In his discussion of music, as in his discussion of poetry, Hegel does not stress the historical development of the art. Such an admission does not imply that Hegel believed an historical analysis of

music was impossible. However, he admitted that he was "no expert in this sphere of musical science" and would, therefore, be unable to do more than "limit myself to more general points of view and a few isolated observations" (*SW*, Glockner, XIV, 131; *PFA*, III, 345).

2. *SW*, Glockner, XIV, 82; *PFA*, III, 295. Hegel noted, however, that painting has one advantage over both music and poetry. The painter can bring the precise scene before us with all its detail. "Hat nun aber der Maler den Vorteil voraus, dass er die bestimmte Scene, indem er sie sinnlich vor die Anschauung im Scheine ihrer wirklichen Realität bringt, in der vollkommensten Einzelnheit ausmalen kann" (*SW*, Glockner, XIV, 83; *PFA*, III, 296).

3. *SW*, Glockner, XIV, 84; *PFA*, III, 297.

4. *Critique of Aesthetic Judgment*, translated by J. C. Meredith, pp. 146 ff. See also Jack Kaminsky, "Kant's Analysis of Aesthetics," *Kant-Studien*, 50 (1958-1959), pp. 77-88.

5. *SW*, Glockner, XIV, 128; *PFA*, III, 341.

6. *SW*, Glockner, XIV, 135; *PFA*, III, 349.

7. *SW*, Glockner, XIV, 133; *PFA*, III, 346.

8. "Fur den Musikausdruck eignet sich deshalb auch nur das ganz objektlose Innere, die abstrakte subjektivität als solche" (*SW*, Glockner, XIV, 129; *PFA*, III, 342).

9. "In dieser Rücksicht besteht die eigenthümliche Aufgabe der Musik darin, dass sie jedweden Inhalt nich so für den Geist macht, wie dieser Inhalt als allgemeine Vorstellung im Bewusstsehn liegt, oder als bestimmte aüssere Gestalt für die Auschauung sonst schon vorhanden ist, oder durch die Kunst seine gemässere Erscheinung erhält, sondern in der Weise, in welche er in der Sphäre der subjektiven Innerlichkeit lebendig wird" (*SW*, Glockner, XIV, 143; *PFA*, III, 358).

10. *SW*, Glockner, XIV, 140; *PFA*, III, 354.

11. *SW*, Glockner, XIV, 140; *PFA*, III, 355.

12. *SW*, Glockner, XIV, 143; *PFA*, III, 357.

13. *SW*, Glockner, XIV, 139; *PFA*, III, 354.

14. *SW*, Glockner, XIV, 141-42; *PFA*, III, 356.

15. *SW*, Glockner, XIV, 203; *PFA*, III, 415.

16. *Ibid.*

17. *SW*, Glockner, XIV, 207; *PFA*, III, 419. Hegel, unlike Schopenhauer, was never completely captivated by Rossini. It is certainly not true, as one modern musicologist maintains, that Hegel "could find only ecstatic words" for Rossini. See Paul Henry Lang, *Music in Western Civilization* (New York: W. W. Norton and Co., 1941), p. 835.

18. *SW*, Glockner, XIV, 147; *PFA*, III, 362.

19. "Da nun die Zeit und nicht die Räumlichkeit als solche das wesentliche Element abgiebt, in welchem der Ton in Rücksicht auf seine musikalische Geltung Existenz gewinnt, und die Zeit des Tons zugleich die des Subjekts ist, so dringt der Ton, schon dieser Grundlage nach, in das Selbst ein, fasst dasselbe seinem einfachsten Dasehn nach, und setzt das Ich durch die zeitliche Bewegung und deren Rhythmus in Bewegung" (*SW*, Glockner, XIV, 151; *PFA*, III, 365).

20. *SW*, Glockner, XIV, 145; *PFA*, III, 360.

21. *SW*, Glockner, XIV, 178; *PFA*, III, 391.

22. *SW*, Glockner, XIV, 179; *PFA*, III, 392.

23. *SW*, Glockner, XIV, 161-62; *PFA*, III, 375.

24. *SW*, Glockner, XIV, 156; *PFA*, III, 370.

25. *Ibid.*

26. *SW*, Glockner, XIV, 165; *PFA*, III, 379.

27. *SW*, Glockner, XIV, 165; *PFA*, III, 378.

28. *SW*, Glockner, XIV, 193; *PFA*, III, 406.

29. *SW*, Glockner, XIV, 194; *PFA*, III, 406.

30. *SW*, Glockner, XIV, 168; *PFA*, III, 381.

31. *SW*, Glockner, XIV, 170; *PFA*, III, 383.

32. *Ibid.*

33. *Ibid.*

34. *SW*, Glockner, XIV, 173-74; *PFA*, III, 386.

Chapter VIII. THE ROMANTIC STAGE OF ART: POETRY

1. *SW*, Glockner, XIV, 222; *PFA*, IV, 5.

2. *Ibid.*

3. "Schon jeder Halm, jeder Baum hat in diesem Sinne seine Geschichte, eine Veränderung, Folge und abgeschlossene Totalität unterschiedener Zustände. Mehr noch ist diess im Gebiete des Giestes der Fall, der als wirklicher erscheinender Geist erschöpfend nur kann dargestellt werden, wenn er uns als solch ein Verlauf vor die Vorstellung kommt" (*SW*, Glockner, XIV, 224; *PFA*, IV, 7). However, Hegel believed that certain kinds of subtle emotions which are observable in a facial expression can be adequately depicted only by the painter.

4. *SW*, Glockner, XIV, 226; *PFA*, IV, 9.

5. *Ibid.*

6. *SW*, Glockner, XIV, 227; *PFA*, IV, 10. For Croce such translation was impossible. "Indeed, every translation either diminishes and spoils, or it creates a new expression" (*Aesthetic*, translated by D. Ainslie, p. 68).

7. *SW*, Glockner, XIV, 229; *PFA*, IV, 12. Hegel, like Plato and

later Croce, seemed to conceive of the art product as no more than an imitation of the idea conceived by the artist. (See Croce's *Aesthetic*, translated by D. Ainslie, pp. 12 ff.) The artist first creates a particular idea or image and then implants it on his material medium. But both Dewey and Collingwood, who were also influenced by Hegel, rejected this view. They argued that the artistic product is not a material duplicate of an idea. On the contrary, the art product develops out of a combination of vague and unformulated ideas which attain form as they are used in a material substance. See R. G. Collingwood, *Principles of Art* (London: Oxford University Press, 1938), p. 28; John Dewey, *Art as Experience* (New York: Minton, Balch and Co., 1934) , p. 53.

8. *SW*, Glockner, XIV, 231; *PFA*, IV, 13.

9. *SW*, Glockner, XIV, 233;*PFA*, IV, 16.

10. "So ist sie die allgemeinste und ausgebreiteste Lehrerin des Menschengeschlechts gewesen und ist est noch" (*SW*, Glockner, XIV, 238; *PFA*, IV, 21) .

11. *SW*, Glockner, XIV, 239; *PFA*, IV, 22.

12. *Ibid.*

13. "Nicht die Sache und deren praktische Existenz, sondern das Bilden und Reden ist der Zweck der Poesie. Sie hat begonnen, als der Mensch es unternahm sich auszusprechen; das Gesprochene ist ihr nur deswegen da, um ausgesprochen zu sehn. Wenn der Mensch selbst mitten innerhalb der praktischen Thätigkeit und Noth einmal zur theoretischen Sammlung übergeht und sich mittheilt, so tritt sogleich ein gebildeter Ausdruck, ein Anklang an das Poetische ein" (*SW*, Glockner, XIV, 239-40; *PFA*, IV, 22-23) .

14. *SW*, Glockner, XIV, 242; *PFA*, IV, 25.

15. *SW*, Glockner, XIV, 277; *PFA*, IV, 59. The poverty of human perception became the basis of T. E. Hulme's argument that art makes us actually perceive what is presented to us. "My perception runs in certain moulds. Things have been classified with a view to the use I can make of them. It is this classification I perceive rather than the real shape of things. I hardly see an object, but merely notice what class it belongs to—what ticket I ought to apply to it" (Quoted from Hulme's *Speculations* in *The Problems of Aesthetics*, edited by Eliseo Vivas and Murray Krieger [New York: Rinehart and Co., 1953], p. 133) .

16. *SW*, Glockner, XIV, 277; *PFA*, IV, 59.

17. *Ibid.*

18. *SW*, Glockner, XIV, 252; *PFA*, IV, 34. For some contemporary criticism and analysis of the conception of organic unity see the following: Harold Osborne, *Aesthetics and Criticism* (New York:

Philosophical Library, 1955), pp. 218 ff.; C. I. Lewis, *An Analysis of Knowledge and Valuation* (La Salle, Illinois: Open Court Publishing Co., 1946), pp. 476 ff.; Stephen C. Pepper, *The Basis of Criticism in the Arts* (Cambridge, Mass.: Harvard University Press, 1949), pp. 74 ff.

19. *SW*, Glockner, XIV, 250; *PFA*, IV, 32.

20. *SW*, Glockner, XIV, 254; *PFA*, IV, 36.

21. *Ibid.*

22. *SW*, Glockner, XIV, 259-60; *PFA*, IV, 41.

23. *SW*, Glockner, XIV, 269; *PFA*, IV, 51.

24. *SW*, Glockner, XIV, 273; *PFA*, IV, 55. But, of course, Hegel overlooks the work of such young artists as Byron, Shelley, and Keats.

25. *SW*, Glockner, XIV, 288; *PFA*, IV, 69.

26. *Ibid.*

27. *Ibid.*

28. *SW*, Glockner, XIV, 291; *PFA*, IV, 72.

29. *SW*, Glockner, XIV, 286; *PFA*, IV, 67.

30. *SW*, Glockner, XIV, 289; *PFA*, IV, 71.

31. *SW*, Glockner, XIV, 293; *PFA*, IV, 75.

32. *SW*, Glockner, XIV, 300; *PFA*, IV, 80.

33. *Ibid.*

34. *SW*, Glockner, XIV, 300; *PFA*, IV, 81.

35. "Nach dieser Seite hin hat sich der Reim nicht zufällig nur in der romantischen Poesie ausgebildet, sondern ist ihr nothwendig gewesen. Das Bedürfniss der Seele, sich selbst zur vernehmen, hebt sich voller, heraus und befriedigt sich in dem Gleichklingen des Reims, das gegen die fest geregelte Zeitmessung gleichgültig macht, und nur darauf hinarbeitet, uns durch Wiederkehr der ähnlichen Klänge zu uns selbst zurückzuführen" (*SW*, Glockner, XIV, 304; *PFA*, IV, 85).

36. *SW*, Glockner, XIV, 327; *PFA*, IV, 107.

37. *SW*, Glockner, XIV, 331; *PFA*, IV, 110.

38. "Die gesammte Weltanschauung und Objektivität eines Volks geistes, in ihrer sich objektivirenden Gestalt als wirkliches Begebniss vorübergeführt, macht deshalb den Inhalt und die Form des eigentlich Epischen aus" (*SW*, Glockner, XIV, 331; *PFA*, IV, 111).

39. *SW*, Glockner, XIV, 332; *PFA*, IV, 112.

40. *Ibid.*

41. *SW*, Glockner, XIV, 333; *PFA*, IV, 112.

42. *SW*, Glockner, XIV, 346; *PFA*, IV, 124.

43. *SW*, Glockner, XIV, 346; *PFA*, IV, 125.

44. *Ibid.*

45. *Ibid.*

46. *SW*, Glockner, XIV, 334; *PFA*, IV, 113.
47. *Ibid.*
48. *SW*, Glockner, XIV, 337; *PFA*, IV, 116.
49. *SW*, Glockner, XIV, 349; *PFA*, IV, 127-28.
50. *SW*, Glockner, XIV, 348; *PFA*, IV, 127.
51. *SW*, Glockner, XIV, 349; *PFA*, IV, 128.
52. "Der Sinn des Rechts und der Billigkeit, die Sitte, das Gemüth, der Charakter muss im Gegentheil als ihr alleiniger Ursprung und ihr Stütze erscheinen" (*SW*, Glockner, XIV, 341; *PFA*, IV, 120).
53. *SW*, Glockner, XIV, 354; *PFA*, IV, 132-33.
54. *SW*, Glockner, XIV, 355; *PFA*, IV, 133.
55. *Ibid.*
56. *SW*, Glockner, XIV, 361; *PFA*, IV, 139.
57. *SW*, Glockner, XIV, 363; *PFA*, IV, 141.
58. *SW*, Glockner, XIV, 366; *PFA*, IV, 144. A. C. Bradley, however, has argued that Hegel's theory of poetry does not do adequate justice to the significance of fate. See "Hegel's Theory of Tragedy," *Oxford Lectures on Poetry* (2d ed.; London: Macmillan Co., 1909), pp. 82-83.
59. *SW*, Glockner, XIV, 368-69; *PFA*, IV, 146.
60. "Die schönste Mitte hingegen vermag die griechische Poesie auch in dieser Rücksicht zu halten, da sie sowohl ihren Göttern als auch ihren Helden und Menschen, der ganzen Grundanschauung nach, eine wechselseitig ungestörte Kraft und Freiheit selbstständiger Individualität geben kann" (*SW*, Glockner, XIV, 369; *PFA*, IV, 146).
61. *SW*, Glockner, XIV, 370; *PFA*, IV, 148.
62. *SW*, Glockner, XIV, 371; *PFA*, IV, 149.
63. *SW*, Glockner, XIV, 372; *PFA*, IV, 150.
64. *Ibid.*
65. *Ibid.*
66. *SW*, Glockner, XIV, 382; *PFA*, IV, 159.
67. *SW*, Glockner, XIV, 383; *PFA*, IV, 159.
68. *SW*, Glockner, XIV, 384; *PFA*, IV, 161. Thus, for Hegel, one of the most important characteristics of the hero is that he has a disinterested interest in himself. He is interested in preserving himself from harm in order to carry through his task and the will of the gods, but he does not make his life his most precious possession.
69. *SW*, Glockner, XIV, 419; *PFA*, IV, 193.
70. *SW*, Glockner, XIV, 444; *PFA*, IV, 215.
71. *Ibid.*
72. *SW*, Glockner, XIV, 424; *PFA*, IV, 197.
73. *SW*, Glockner, XIV, 428; *PFA*, IV, 201.
74. *SW*, Glockner, XIV, 441; *PFA*, IV, 213.

75. *SW*, Glockner, XIV, 441; *PFA*, IV, 212.

76. *SW*, Glockner, XIV, 435; *PFA*, IV, 207.

77. *SW*, Glockner, XIV, 460; *PFA*, IV, 230.

78. In fact, Hegel believed that even though assonance, alliteration, and rhyme do appear in the epic, their poetic use is primarily "limited to the province of the Lyric" (*SW*, Glockner, XIV, 452; *PFA*, IV, 223).

79. *SW*, Glockner, XIV, 480; *PFA*, IV, 249.

80. "Was wir deshalb vor uns sehen sind die zu lebendigen Characteren und konfliktreichen Situationen individualisirten Zwecke, in ihrem sich Zeigen und Behaupten, Einwirken und Bestimmen gegeneinander;—alles in Augenblicklichkeit wechselseitiger Aeusserungsowie das in sich selbst begründete Endresultat dieses ganzen sich bewegt durchkreuzenden und dennoch zur Ruhe lösenden menschlichen Getriebes in Wollen und Vollbringen" (*SW*, Glockner, XIV, 480; *PFA*, IV, 249).

81. *SW*, Glockner, XIV, 556; *PFA*, IV, 324.

82. *SW*, Glockner, XIV, 557; *PFA*, IV, 324-25.

83. *SW*, Glockner, XIV, 558; *PFA*, IV, 326.

84. *SW*, Glockner, XIV, 485; *PFA*, IV, 254.

85. *SW*, Glockner, XIV, 485-86; *PFA*, IV, 255.

86. *SW*, Glockner, XIV, 486; *PFA*, IV, 255.

87. *SW*, Glockner, XIV, 508; *PFA*, IV, 276. I. A. Richards has denied that truth has any significance for the work of art. "In the reading of *Lear,* what facts verifiable by science or accepted or believed in as we accept and believe in ascertaining facts are relevant? None whatever" (*Principles of Literary Criticism* [New York: Harcourt, Brace and Co., 1924], p. 282). Similar statements are to be found in contemporary positivistic literature. See, for example, *Aesthetics and Language,* edited by William Elton (New York: Philosophical Library, 1954). Hegel, of course, would have considered these views preposterous. The artist is as much open to the charge of falsehood and inconsistency as are natural and social scientists.

88. *SW*, Glockner, XIV, 508; *PFA*, IV, 276-77.

89. This is not a violation of the Aristotelian dictum. Aristotle maintains that the tragic action should not exceed a day, but he does not mention the unity of place. Moreover, the *Eumenides* of Aeschylus and the *Ajax* of Sophocles do have changes of place.

90. *SW*, Glockner, XIV, 489; *PFA*, IV, 258.

91. *SW*, Glockner, XIV, 489; *PFA*, IV, 259.

92. See especially Edward Bullough, "Psychical Distance as

Factor in Art and Aesthetic Principle," *British Journal of Psychology,* 5 (1912-1913), 87-118.

93. *SW,* Glockner, XIV, 491; *PFA,* IV, 260.

94. "Nun erhält zwar in der empirischen Wirklichkeit jede Handlung mannigfaltige Voraussetzungen, so dass es sich schwer bestimmen lässt, an welchem Punkte der eigentliche Anfang zu finden seh; insofern aber die dramatische Handlung wesentlich auf einer bestimmten Kollision beruht, wird der gemässe Ausgangspunkt in der Situation liegen, aus welcher sich jener Konflikt, obschon er noch nicht hervorgebrochen ist, dennoch im weitern Verlaufe entwickeln muss. Das Ende dagegen wird dann erreicht sehn, wenn sich die Auflösung des Zwiespalts und der Verwickelung in jeder Rücksicht zu Stande gebracht hat" (*SW,* Glockner, XIV, 494; *PFA,* IV, 263).

95. Pathos, according to Hegel, is an emotion which appears when a man feels himself to be bound by two contradictory but ethical demands. Since this sort of ethical conflict signifies precisely that conflict which man, *qua* man, ought to engage in, Hegel believed that any spectator of such activity would immediately receive a similar emotional reaction. See *SW,* Glockner, XIV, 496; *SW,* Lasson, Xa, 316; *PFA,* I, 308; *PFA,* IV, 265.

96. *SW,* Glockner, XIV, 502; *PFA,* IV, 271.

97. *Ibid.*

98. *SW,* Glockner, XIV, 504; *PFA,* IV, 273.

99. *SW,* Glockner, XIV, 506; *PFA,* IV, 274.

100. *SW,* Glockner, XIV, 515; *PFA,* IV, 282-83.

101. *SW,* Glockner, XIV, 516; *PFA,* IV, 284.

102. *SW,* Glockner, XIV, 519; *PFA,* IV, 287.

103. *SW,* Glockner, XIV, 521; *PFA,* IV, 289.

104. See also A. C. Bradley's remarks on this point in "Hegel's Theory of Tragedy," *op. cit.,* pp. 74-75.

105. *SW,* Glockner, XIV, 566; *PFA,* IV, 334-35.

106. *SW,* Glockner, XIV, 568; *PFA,* IV, 337.

107. *SW,* Glockner, XIV, 569; *PFA,* IV, 338.

108. *SW,* Glockner, XIV, 562; *PFA,* IV, 330.

109. *SW,* Glockner, XIV, 574; *PFA,* IV, 343.

Chapter IX. CONCLUSION AND CRITICISM

1. Harold Osborne, *Aesthetics and Criticism* (New York: Philosophical Library, 1955), p. 98.

2. Arnold Hauser, *Social History of Art* (London: Routledge and Kegan Paul, 1951).

3. Osborne, *op. cit.,* Chap. IX.

4. "These three events—the so-called Revival of Learning, the flourishing of the Fine Arts and the discovery of America and of the passage to India by the Cape—may be compared with that *blush of dawn* which after long storms first betokens the return of a bright and glorious day. This day is the day of Universality, which breaks upon the world after the long, eventful, and terrible night of the Middle Ages—a day which is distinguished by science, art, and inventive impulse—that is, by the noblest and highest (*The Philosophy of History,* translated by J. Sibree [New York: P. F. Collier and Son, 1902], p. 512).

5. *SW*, Glockner, XIV, 111; *PFA*, III, 323.

6. *SW*, Glockner, XIII, 402; *PFA*, III, 157.

INDEX

INDEX